MOST PLANETS WILL NEVER HAVE LIFE

A GUIDE TO JOYFUL PARENTING IN THE FACE OF BIOSPHERE COLLAPSE

by Kunal Dalal

Most Planets Will Never Even Have Life:
A Guide to Joyful Parenting in the Face of Biosphere Collapse

Published by LKZ Press

Printed in United States

ISBN: 979-8-9866814-5-0

Table of Contents

Introduction

When I was a high school Biology teacher, I abolished Earth Day in my classroom.

Not because I didn't believe in the urgency of the crisis around climate change, but rather because I believed it was in fact too urgent. I was a teacher in an alternative school, where students expelled or suspended from the traditional schools spent their days.

We were still showing pictures of polar bears and rainforests to Black and brown kids living amongst poverty and violence, all while they were being criminalized simply for being Black, or because their parents didn't speak English very well. I was looking at these kids and thinking, they do not care about polar bears and rainforests. And based on how much they fight daily simply to feel ok as a human, why should they?

Because it's not about saving the Earth. If you looked out of the window 4 billion years ago, you'd see a flaming ball of molten rock. And in 4 billion years if you look out of the window you'll see a flaming ball of molten rock. No matter what we do, the Earth will continue, it doesn't care that we exist.

What we do have, is we happen to live in this tiny sliver of time when we get to have a relationship to an Earth that brims with the most improbable beauty and magic of life. We get to have a relationship with the lion, the dragonfly, the elephant and the whale, and appreciate this absolutely unlikely, and infinitely beautiful event called life.

We also get to have a relationship with ourselves. In just this tiny sliver of time on our planet we've created works of beauty that are barely believable, from the ancient artwork in the caves of Lascaux, to the heart-rending hymns of indigenous Americans. We've created Beethoven's symphonies and we've created the *Before* series. The Taj Mahal wasn't built in a day, but it was built. And it was built because we have been so stupidly lucky to have a relationship to our Earth.

And so what we're really trying to save is not Earth, but rather our own humanity. The humanity that created works of art that can bring the hardest of us to gasping tears, the humanity that learned how the most distant stars in the universe could guide us across massive oceans on our tiny little blue dot. The humanity of a brand new mother holding her baby and imagining the relationship this new life might have with the Earth around her. That's what we're trying to save. That is the purpose of caring.

So back to wanting to abolish Earth Day back in my classroom, I wanted us to celebrate Humanity Day. A day where we dedicated time to try and reintroduce ourselves to that humanity. We likely cannot quantify what we are at risk of losing, but we know it is big. Because let's truly embrace our reality, we are living in an epoch of the Earth's history that is determined by us. We are now, whether we want to be or not, stewards for all life around us. Our decisions will determine what happens to everything.

What a time to be human.

1: The Reality Ahead: Facing Collapse with Open Eyes

"Every man, at some point in his life, is going to lose a battle. He is going to fight and he is going to lose. But what makes him a man, is that in the midst of that battle, he does not lose himself."

-**Coach Taylor, *Friday Night Lights***

There have been a lot of introductions written about the imminent collapse of our long-held ecological stability as well as our entrenched societal order. For decades, authors, scientists, and activists have signaled alarms, woven narratives, and presented cold, hard data. Yet, here we stand, at the precipice, still searching for answers and ways forward. This chapter is not just another doom-laden prophecy, but a sincere attempt to look unflinchingly at the reality we're confronted with.

The Undeniable Signs

All around us, we are bearing witness: escalating temperatures, erratic weather patterns, and diminishing resources. But it isn't just about the tangible shifts in our environment. The changes extend to economic systems, political dynamics, and cultural fabrics. Our world, in many ways, is becoming unrecognizable. We are not discussing a distant possibility anymore; we are living in the midst of it. The underpinnings of what we considered 'normal' are unraveling, and a new, undefined reality is emerging.

As I write this now, in late 2023, we're seeing devastating, almost inconceivable floods in Libya, the US, Canada, Europe, and the list goes on. We're seeing wildfires and bushfires in every continent, most now erupting at a scale and intensity well ahead of scientists' most dire predictions. This is not news to you. I could continue down the list, but I'm sure by the time you're reading this there will be a new set of scarcely imaginable environmental disasters unfolding. So you can write those in the margins if you like, to add to the list.

But I'm going to argue that you'd be wasting your time. Keeping up with news and doom-scrolling have become synonymous in recent years it seems, so why not get your eyeballs looking in a different direction, and look at what remains with a new lens. This is not a drill, this is not practice. We're in this in real time, and we have, within ourselves, the greatest tool on this Earth, human will. I mean, it's our will that bent our environment to this point right? We're pretty damn impressive when we dedicate ourselves. But it starts with a recognition of where we are, and a healthy movement through what that realization means for you and your family.

The Emotional Struggle: Grief and Acceptance

For almost all of us, this recognition brings immense grief. There's a mourning for the world we once knew, the futures we envisioned for ourselves and our children. The pain is deeply emotional and spiritual. It's about coming to terms with the loss of dreams and expectations. But through this grief, there's also an opportunity for acceptance. Acceptance doesn't mean complacency, it means understanding our new reality and choosing how we want to engage with it. I'll be repeating this a few times in this chapter.

Denial can be comforting. It offers a temporary respite, a chance to close our eyes and hope everything will be okay when we open them again. But shielding our eyes from the impending and imminent madness robs us of the chance to prepare, adapt, and perhaps, even find joy in the journey ahead. By confronting the truth, by seeking clarity, we reclaim our agency. With this clear-sightedness, there's a unique strength, one that allows us to see beyond and around the challenges, and discover the slivers of light hidden within them.

The Journey Forward

As I delve deeper into this chapter, I will explore these facets of our reality and examine the potential paths before us. I don't promise easy solutions, because there are none. But I will try to offer a perspective, a lens through which you might find humor, resilience, and the will to move forward. In acknowledging the gravity of our situation, we might also open the doors to possibility, creativity, and a deeper connection to our planet and one another.

Shifting Perspectives: From Grief to Guidance

In the face of this overwhelming ecological and societal shift, it's only natural for our first reaction to be one of grief. For parents, this grief is doubly profound, as we grieve not just for ourselves, but for the future of our children. Yet, throughout history, we have demonstrated an unparalleled ability to adapt, evolve, and reinvent. This chapter dives into the transformative process of moving from grief to guidance, from personal loss to parental leadership.

Grief is not a sign of weakness or a descent into helplessness; it's a testament to our love and attachment to everything we've known. For parents, grieving acknowledges the uncertainties we feel about what our children will inherit. This emotional depth becomes the foundation upon which we can build a perspective that actively seeks solutions and new paths for our families.

The Role of Acceptance

In many ways, acceptance is an act of immense bravery, especially for parents. Accepting the potential challenges our children might face feels unimaginable at times, but it's a necessary step toward proactive preparation. By accepting the state of our planet and society at large, we anchor ourselves, and pave the way for our children to grow in an environment of realism and resilience.

The Power of Resilience

Human history is stuffed with examples of societies that have risen from decline, communities that have remade themselves in the aftermath of calamities. Our resilience as a species is one of our most defining traits. As parents, instilling this resilience in our children means teaching them to embrace change, to see adversity as just another part of living, one that must be faced directly, and one that could open up new ways of thinking in the future.

Guidance: The Role of Compassionate Leadership

Grief and acceptance lead us to guidance. In these tumultuous times, the world needs compassionate leaders, and parents are often the first leaders a child ever knows. This leadership begins with self-guidance: understanding our emotions, cultivating resilience, and then extending our insights outward to model a way forward for our children.

Shifting our perspective is not an overnight assignment. It's a journey that requires patience, introspection, and a fair share of courage. For us parents, this journey has that added layer of responsibility, as we shape both our own outlook and that of our children. By embracing this shift, we can illuminate new avenues of action, ensuring that our children are equipped to thrive amidst the changes ahead.

The Grieving Process for the Joyful Collapse Parent

Walking the path of a Joyful Collapse Parent is to first navigate through the familiar stages of grief. This isn't about surrendering to fear; it's about understanding the profound changes we face. I want to walk through these stages as outlined by Elisabeth Kübler-Ross in *On Death and Dying*, which has become a standard text in our understanding of this journey.

Denial & Isolation:
At first, it's tempting for parents to shield themselves and their children from the emerging realities. The belief often is, "Maybe it won't be so bad," or "Perhaps our family won't be affected." This is the protective instinct, grasping for a cocoon of normalcy.

A parent might avoid discussing noticeable changes in the environment or societal shifts with their child. When the child brings up unusual weather patterns or asks why certain resources are scarce, the parent might deflect or offer a simplified answer, hoping to maintain their child's sense of normalcy.

Anger:
Recognition brings a surge of frustration. Parents often wonder, "How did it come to this?" or "Why didn't we act sooner?" The challenge here is to use this energy not for blame, but for action and understanding. For example, upon seeing their child's outdoor activities restricted due to poor air quality or learning about resource shortages in school, a parent's protective instincts flare. They might voice frustration, saying, "Why didn't those in power do more when there was time?" The child, sensing this emotion, might become more alert to the realities but also more anxious.

Bargaining:
While in this phase, parents might think, "If we adopt certain practices, maybe things will turn around," or "Perhaps if we educate our kids on this topic, they'll have a better chance." It's a search for solutions, a desperate quest for a safety net. Parents might promise their child special trips or rewards if they adopt certain sustainable habits or learn specific skills. "If we save enough water this month, we can go camping," or "Let's learn to

grow our own food, it could be fun!" It's a hopeful exchange, an attempt to find a positive spin. In this stage, we parents likely have not fully internalized our present, and so we might still believe just a little more "good" behavior might mean we will be okay.

Depression:
The enormity of what's ahead is unequivocally overwhelming. Parents might feel they're carrying the weight of the world, because in many ways they are. We are uncertain about the future we're facing, and about the future we're crafting for our children.

Observing our child's play—imagining clear skies when it's consistently gray outside—can tug at a parent's heartstrings. My own child's love of wild animals sometimes breaks me in half. I don't know if he'll ever know that world. The stark difference between our children's imagination and reality might lead to moments of sorrow, thinking, "Is this what I'm leaving for them?" Here, it's crucial to remember that sharing these feelings and seeking support is a must, for ourselves and for our kids.

Acceptance:
As I've said multiple times before, acceptance isn't about passive resignation, but about having clarity and purpose. With acceptance, parents can take informed actions, preparing their children for realities that are changing, ensuring they face it with realism and open eyes.

A family camping trip, where parent and child sit under the stars, becomes a moment of truth. The parent, with a mix of sadness and resolve, might share stories of the past and express look for joy in the present. Kids love to hear stories, especially ones filled with vivid images and palpable emotion. Reach deep within yourself to give this to your kids.

Learning from End-of-life Care: A Look at Dr. Atul Gawande

In his profound exploration of end-of-life care in *Being Mortal*, Atul Gawande delves deep into the notion that understanding and preparing for the eventualities of our mortality can lead to a richer, more fulfilled life. As we confront the daunting reality of societal and ecological collapse, parents can find guidance in Gawande's insights, adapting his insights to this batshit crazy time.

Prioritize Quality Over Quantity

Gawande emphasizes the significance of quality of life over simply prolonging it. In the context of our impending global meltdown, it's vital for parents to focus on the quality of moments they create with their children, rather than focusing solely on longevity.

Example for Parents: Instead of investing solely in stockpiling food, consider also creating meaningful traditions. This might mean growing a family garden, where the act of planting, nurturing, and harvesting becomes a cherished memory. In Chapter 5, I go more deeply into some concrete activities that more completely capture this mindset.

Open Conversations About Reality

A recurring theme in the book is the pivotal role of honest conversations about death in the realm of end-of-life care. Gawande says that by confronting and discussing the inevitable – instead of skirting around it – we grant patients the autonomy to make decisions that align with their values, desires, and understanding of life's worth. These discussions empower them to have control over the final chapter of their stories, even when faced with the most challenging decisions.

Drawing a parallel to our larger societal context, the concept can be extended to the necessity of discussing social and environmental collapse with these younger generations. Just as it's imperative to inform patients of their realities, it's equally essential to communicate with children about the world's challenges. However, this must be done with great care, keeping in mind the child's age, maturity, and emotional readiness. Simplifying complex topics without trivializing them, using relatable analogies, or perhaps embedding lessons in stories can make these subjects digestible.

Example for Parents: For younger children, use storybooks about change and adaptation to introduce the topic gently. With older kids, documentaries or news articles can be the starting point for open-ended discussions.

Empower Choices

Gawande highlights that giving patients choices, even small ones, can greatly enhance their sense of purpose and well-being. As we navigate challenging times, it's crucial for children to feel they have agency and can make choices. There will be so much surrounding them that will feel out of control, giving them opportunities to feel otherwise will be important.

Example for Parents: Allow your child to have a say in family decisions related to preparedness. Whether it's choosing the seeds for the garden, picking a skill to learn, or selecting books for the family's emergency kit, these choices matter.

Embrace Interdependence

Gawande observes that, in our later years, the support of community and family becomes paramount. As we face societal changes, the interconnectedness of communities will be vital. I don't know how much apocalypse movies and shows get right, but I can't think of any where family is central.

Example for Parents: Foster a sense of community early on. This might mean forming neighborhood preparedness groups, engaging in community service projects, or simply organizing regular community potlucks.

Cherish Everyday Joys:

In end-of-life care, small joys – like tasting a favorite food or feeling the sun on one's face – become magnified. Similarly, as we approach potential societal upheavals, finding and cherishing daily joys with our children will be invaluable. It may not be Big Macs and trips to Disneyland, but that's okay, we're well past that. Our joys are intimate, personal, and everywhere.

Example for Parents: Create a "Joy Journal" or a "Book of Delights" with your child, where you both record small, daily delights, from the song of a bird to the feel of rain.

Moving Forward: Embracing Reality with Compassion and Clarity

As we close this introductory chapter of the book, I find myself reflecting on the immensity of the journey that we've embarked on together. The looming shadow of collapse, with its intricate layers of societal and ecological uncertainties, is overwhelming. Much like the impending end-of-life moment that each of us will grapple with, acknowledging the vast impact of collapse requires its own emotional voyage. However, accepting this journey, marked by denial, anger, and eventual acceptance, can lead to both understanding and empowerment.

At first glance, it might seem absurd to juxtapose Atul Gawande's thoughts on individual end-of-life care with guiding healthy, vivacious children through the early stages of life. The two scenarios appear so incredibly different. End-of-life care discussions evoke images of frailty, finality, and reflection, while childhood is typically associated with vibrancy, potential, and unbridled energy. However, in the face of profound societal change, perhaps these seemingly disparate situations might have more in common than we think.

Gawande's central tenet emphasizes understanding and valuing the quality of life over merely its duration. His work in *Being Mortal* highlights the importance of meaningful conversations, acceptance, and a clear-eyed view of the inevitable, ensuring that individuals live their final days in accordance with their values and desires. When we transpose this perspective on to early childhood in a rapidly changing society, we encounter a poignant parallel.

Today's children are coming of age in a world that is, in many ways, unrecognizable from the one in which their parents or grandparents grew up. Environmental challenges, technological disruptions, and societal shifts are changing the narrative of what it means to grow up. By channeling Gawande's philosophy, parents can prepare their children by having open, age-appropriate conversations about what is happening around them.

Just as Gawande advocates for cherishing every moment in the twilight of life, so can parents teach their children to appreciate the beauty of every day, even amidst the mess we're in. In reality, it's how we all should live life everyday.

I hope that this first chapter has laid a foundation of understanding and offered some space for our collective grief. As we delve deeper into subsequent sections, my aspiration remains: to offer tools, insights, and perhaps most importantly, a sense of shared purpose. It's my sincerest wish that as we continue this exploration together, you'll find something of value to carry with you on your own unique journey.

2: The Philosophy of Joyful Collapse Parenting

"Let your life lightly dance on the edges of Time like dew on the tip of a leaf."

-Rabindranath Tagore

Learning from Two Masters: Dalai Lama and Archbishop Desmond Tutu

When I think about living joyfully, I often go back to the works of these two brilliant and compassionate minds. Each person, on his own, offers the kind of insight that we really need in our current moment. But, then they decided to come together to write *The Book of Joy*, and I can't help but see the power of this work in the context of collapse preparation. They outlined their *Eight Pillars of Joy*, and I think looking at some of these pillars, in our context, can add a layer of peaceful wisdom to our work.

Perspective: The power of perspective is one we delved into in the previous chapter, moving from a framework of grief to one of guidance. Joyful Collapse Parenting involves recognizing that while we may all face significant challenges, it is our perspective that grounds our children's worldview. By framing preparation as an adventure and not a macabre chore, we teach our children to approach challenges with curiosity and resilience. Building upon the shift we discussed earlier we're not going to ignore reality but choose which lens to view it through. Drawing upon past insights, we can guide our children to see opportunities where otherwise one might only see obstacles.

Humility: It's an incredible thought, that in our universe, most planets form and disintegrate, never even graced with the accident of life. Yet, here we are, exploding with life, experiences, and hardly believable realities like consciousness, imagination and wonder. For me, this realization brings up a profound sense of humility. Our lives are ephemeral moments that embody the rarity and beauty of existence. In acknowledging our tiny yet significant place in the cosmic chaos, we teach our children to cherish the gift of this life amidst the boundless–*and mostly lifeless*–expanse of space.

Humor: Humor is not an act, it's not making a well-timed joke. Humor is a way of walking through the world. It's one where you don't (and frankly can't) take yourself too seriously, and accept that all of our limitations are what make us glorious, and sometimes unexpectedly hilarious. True humor is a lens through which we view our existence. In the comedy of our imperfections and our many human quirks, we find a shared experience that's both gloriously profound and undeniably hilarious.

Even the fact that we're preparing for a biosphere collapse is completely absurd. The idea of meticulously planning for the unpredictable, of stockpiling and strategizing against the unknown, is funny. As Joyful Collapse Parents, we teach our kids that it's not just okay but essential to laugh at our missteps, embrace our unique quirks, and find the joke in the everyday—especially in the face of the uncertain future.

Acceptance: Central to Joyful Collapse Parenting is the acceptance of the realities ahead. Instead of drinking from the beer stein of false hope, we acknowledge the world as it is head-on. This acceptance becomes the foundation upon which we build a plan, a vision, and a constructive mindset to what lies ahead.

"Acceptance," the Dalai Lama noted, "does not mean passivity." I'd listen to that guy. Joyful Collapse Parents don't resign to the future, we accept and adapt, crafting a vision anchored in joy and tireless forward momentum.

Forgiveness: As we prepare, we may feel guilt for the future we're passing on to our children. It's crucial to teach our children the art of forgiveness, both towards others and themselves. This pillar serves as a reminder that it's okay to fail, as long as we rise again with grace and purpose. And as parents from a previous generation, we have to forgive ourselves. We were there when change could have been made, and maybe we feel like we didn't scream loudly enough.

But for almost all of us, this was well and truly out of our hands. We could have changed every incandescent bulb, driven less, biked more, but we're just individuals up against a seven billion person juggernaut. In that time, many poorer nations have improved their life expectancy, reduced infant mortality, and massive swathes of people have been lifted out of poverty. This was a false choice from the start, and that is okay.

Archbishop Tutu said, "To forgive is the best form of self-interest." Embracing forgiveness means we extend our forgiveness further, to those in positions of capitalist power who ignored the alarms and pleas to protect our biosphere. It's easy to harbor resentment for missed opportunities or for actions that accelerated the challenges we face today. However, by teaching our children the power of forgiveness, we show them the importance of letting go of blame, ensuring they not only move past these historical grievances but also channel their energies into a proactive, positive present. This approach allows them to contextualize history's mistakes without being tethered to its burdens.

Gratitude: Even in a world facing upheaval, there are countless daily blessings. Cultivating a sense of gratitude in our children helps them see the beauty that still exists, from the chirping of birds to the warmth of a shared meal. It's about focusing on the abundance that remains, not just on what might be dwindling. It starts with embracing the singular thing that is life, and then celebrating the connections we are able to make during our time on Earth.

Compassion: Compassion becomes even more vital in times of change. By instilling a sense of compassion in our children, we're not only preparing them for the future but ensuring they become caretakers of both the planet and its people. Joyful Collapse Parenting emphasizes the importance of standing together, helping each other, and understanding the shared human experience.

Generosity: In preparing for the future, there will be moments to hold close and moments to give freely. By teaching our children the value of generosity, we ensure they not only look out for their well-being but also extend a hand to others in need. Generosity, in the end, binds communities and creates a network of shared hope and joy. Some examples of preparing for collapse can look very selfish. Underground bunkers guarded by armed A.I.-powered robots for the wealthy, amassing an arsenal of firearms for others.

But what is this really modeling for our kids? Their money can buy them destructive tools to perhaps live a little longer, and sometimes that can make me angry. When I go there, I remind myself that they are going to die, same as me. But their last years will be spent stressing over their material possessions, and I'll spend mine with nothing to lose but with everything to gain from the laughter of my kids and the simplicity of where my joy will come from. I'm sure this is just another defense mechanism I've constructed, but in this lifetime, all we have is what we've built in our own minds and hearts.

Sure, if we could live forever, violently protecting our immortality would make sense. But all of our times will come, and when it does, living in the spirit of generosity is what will give our lives meaning, not soul-voiding self-interest.

The Essence of Joyful Preparedness

The philosophy of joyful preparedness is not new; it's simply a reawakening of ancient human values. It's about preparing our children, first for survival, and then for a life rich in experiences, emotions, and connections. It's not about bunkers and hoarding but about resilience, adaptability, and finding beauty amid chaos.

Daniel Levitin, in his book *The Organized Mind*, mentions that our brains aren't built for the 21st century but were molded for our ancient ancestors who thrived on creativity, storytelling, and the basics of human connection. We're wired for the elements of humanity that have been our bedrock for millennia: compassion, love, music, art, curiosity, creativity, laughter, and storytelling.

Compassion and Love: We often think of compassion as an emotional state of being, but this emotion is actually an evolutionary trait. It's what binds communities together, creating a network of support. As the Dalai Lama and Desmond Tutu elaborate in *The Book of Joy*, compassion and love are essential components of true joy, becoming even more crucial in times of uncertainty. By fostering these feelings, we not only prepare our children to face challenges but to build bridges, understanding, and community.

Music and Art: Music and art are universal languages of the soul. In *This Is Your Brain on Music*, Levitin describes how music is deeply rooted in our neural pathways, shaping our experiences and memories. Art offers a medium to express, reflect, and interpret everything around us. They are essential tools for emotional expression, healing, and understanding. It's an incredible example of the depth of the kind of life our Earth has fostered, a species that can be so moved by the melodies and the art we can create and appreciate.

Curiosity: When I was a teacher, I would often hear colleagues complain about disruptive students, *"I don't want the kids that don't want to learn to distract from the kids that want to learn."*

I have a strong counter to that. There is no such thing as a kid that doesn't want to learn. That is a null set. We may not be teaching those kids in a way that they find engaging, but they certainly don't want to learn. And that's one of our biggest challenges, to keep our kids' curiosity strong by keeping their eyes wide, and sharing in their delight as they discover all the things that they will discover..

Creativity: Creativity is a sophisticated intellectual method of problem-solving. Ken Robinson, in his famous TED Talk "Schools kill creativity", mentions the need to redefine human capacity to meet the unprecedented challenges we face. By fostering creativity, we equip our kids with the ability to connect pragmatism and imagination, helping them find unique solutions to thrive in an uncharted global paradigm.

Laughter: There's a reason why laughter is called the best medicine. Beyond its physiological benefits, it offers a momentary reprieve from the harshest realities, binding people together with a shared cackle. Mark Twain (who else?) noted, "The human race has one really effective weapon, and that is laughter." I'll go more in depth about the importance of laughter in Chapter 5, and speak directly to how laughter kept many people sane when the world around them was falling apart.

Storytelling: From ancient campfires to modern-day podcasts, storytelling remains a powerful medium of education and connection. It's through stories that lessons are passed, wisdom is shared, and cultures are preserved. Jonathan Gottschall wrote a whole book about it, *The Storytelling Animal*, where he explores how humans are creatures that crave story, and in our building of internal and external narratives, lies one of our greatest strengths.

Neurologist, author, and Holocaust survivor Viktor E. Frankl said in his profound and life-affirming book *Man's Search for Meaning*, "Between stimulus and response, there is a space. In that space is our power to choose our response. In our response lies our growth and our freedom." You're here because you want to choose joy.

The Tale of Sango: From Self-Inflicted Destruction to Redemption

Within the rich tradition of Yoruba mythology, Sango is a compelling figure, embodying the dance between power and responsibility. Crowned as the king of the ancient Oyo Empire, Sango wielded great political might and also supernatural prowess, being the god of thunder and lightning. His double-headed axe symbolized the intensity of his powers, allowing him to summon storms at will.

Yet, like many tales of great power, Sango's is also marked by tragedy. One fateful day, in a fit of rage, he conjured a storm so fierce that it inadvertently razed his palace to the ground and claimed the lives of his beloved family. This heart-shattering incident, borne of his own unchecked powers, plunged Sango into an abyss of guilt and self-reflection.

Overwhelmed by remorse for the devastation he had brought on his own kin, Sango contemplated ending his life, hoping to find escape in oblivion. However, a transformative journey awaited him. Rather than giving in to despair, Sango chose the path of redemption. He learned the delicate balance between strength and restraint, realizing that true power lay not in displays of his might but in controlled, compassionate leadership.

Gradually, Sango transformed from a tempestuous god to a revered deity, teaching his followers the values of balanced power, humility, and introspection. As the god of both thunder (symbolizing destruction) and drumming (representing creation), Sango's tale underscores the coexistence of creation and destruction, of despair and retribution.

Sango: A Metaphor for Approaching Collapse

This tale of Sango can offer a meaningful metaphor when considering the approach to collapse. His story, marked by power, tragedy, remorse, and redemption, offers valuable insights on our journey through the complex landscape of societal and ecological change.

Unchecked Power and Consequences:

Sango's Story: With his immense power and temper, Sango inadvertently causes the destruction of his own palace and the demise of his family. His uncontrolled emotions and abilities lead to unintentional devastation.

Collapse Parallel: Unchecked industrialization, relentless pursuit of growth, and disregard for ecological balance have set us on a path of nearly assured devastation. Like Sango's unintended consequences, humanity's unbridled actions have placed us on the precipice of ecological and societal collapse.

Deep Remorse and Introspection:

Sango's Journey: Following the catastrophe, Sango is consumed by remorse. This sorrow pushes him into a period of introspection, where he grapples with the weight of his actions.

Collapse Insight: As the signs of impending collapse become clearer, there's a collective sorrow and guilt, especially for the choices of past generations. It's essential to confront these feelings, reflect on past actions, and seek understanding.

Sango's Redemption: From his remorse, Sango learns the importance of balanced leadership. He learns to rein in his temper, lead with both power and compassion, and becomes a revered figure in Yoruba mythology.

Collapse Parallel: In the face of impending challenges, there's an opportunity for redemption. By acknowledging past mistakes, societies can work towards a more balanced coexistence with nature. The balance between technological advancement and ecological preservation becomes crucial, much like Sango's balance of power and compassion.

Embracing Dualities:

Sango's Dual Nature: As a god of both thunder (destructive) and drumming (creative), Sango embodies duality. His story underscores the coexistence of creation and destruction, joy and sorrow.

Collapse Insight: Facing collapse requires us to embrace dualities. While there's the valid grief of loss, there's also the joy of reconnection, of communities banding together, and of rediscovering simpler pleasures.

The Power of Second Chances:

Sango's Legacy: Despite his initial fall from grace, Sango is given a second chance, which he seizes to transform and guide his followers.

Collapse Parallel: Even as we stare at the potential collapse, there's still time and opportunity to chart a new course. By learning from the past and adopting a balanced approach, there's a chance to mitigate the harshest impacts and craft a future imbued with wisdom from our mistakes.

There are many ancient and traditional stories of destruction and redemption from cultures spanning the entirety of human time and space here on Earth. And while there are great lessons to learn from them, there are also lessons to be learned from more contemporary examples.

The Heartbreaking and Inspirational Guido from *A Beautiful Life*

I want to look at a character from a film released not long ago, because I think there are wonderful and terrible parallels with what we are faced with as parents today.

Guido Orefice, the central character in Roberto Benigni's heart-wrenching film *Life is Beautiful,* is a Jewish father imprisoned with his son, Giosuè, in a Nazi concentration camp during World War II. Faced with an unimaginable situation and the instinctual desire to protect his son from the horrific realities of the camp, Guido devises an imaginative game. He tells Giosuè that the camp is a unique competition, and the winner will receive a real tank as the grand prize. To earn points in this game, they must abide by certain "rules," such as hiding from the guards or being silent – tactics that in reality are meant to keep Giosuè safe from the Nazis' deadly intentions.

If you have young children who you feel may not be ready for the real gravity of what is happening, we can learn a lot from Guido's gameplay. The primary motive behind this charade is to shield his son from the trauma and terror surrounding them, preserving Giosuè's innocence in a world gone mad. Guido's imaginative game is a testament to the lengths a parent will go to protect their child, even in the most dire circumstances. Through humor, creativity, and unwavering love, Guido tries to create a buffer against the camp's horrors, turning grim survival into a child's adventure. This narrative strategy serves as both a coping mechanism and a light amid profound darkness.

Guido Orefice's poignant playfulness in the concentration camp to shield his son from horror draws an emotional parallel to the concept of creating games around preparing for societal collapse. In both scenarios, games become a strategy for resilience, transforming the narrative of pain into one of empowerment and love.

How can I learn about my own parenting from Guido?

Preservation of Innocence: Just as Guido sought to keep the innocence of his child intact amidst the nightmare of the concentration camp, creating light-hearted games around collapse preparation can keep younger generations bright-eyed and manage anxiety. This childlike wonder and imagination can become a powerful tool in the face of grim realities.

Constructive Engagement: By turning preparation into a game, tasks that might seem daunting or depressing are reframed as challenges to be overcome. This mirrors Guido's approach, where dire circumstances are presented as obstacles in a grand game. The mindset shift from "survival" to "game" makes the process more engaging and less overwhelming.

Building Resilience: Through games, children can develop practical skills and knowledge without being heavily burdened by the gravity of why they're learning them. This mimics Guido teaching his son how to hide or stay silent, all packaged in the guise of scoring game points.

Fostering Community and Connection: Games are communal by nature. Preparing for the future through shared games can create a sense of community, much like Guido and Giosuè's strengthened bond. In times of distress, this unity becomes invaluable.

Empowerment: Games often have objectives, scores, or achievements. This gives participants, especially children, a sense of accomplishment and progress, countering feelings of helplessness or passivity.

The infinite heart and soul of Guido's tactics and the strategy of playful collapse preparation both stem from the same profound love and protective instinct. They emphasize the human capacity for creativity and adaptability, even in the face of the most foreboding circumstances.

The Peril of the Perpetual Smile: A Cautionary Note from Victor Hugo's Gwynplaine

In the midst of collapse, the role of a Joyful Collapse Parent may seem akin to Guido from *Life is Beautiful*, however there's another, more insidious side to embodying the joyful, playful persona to protect your children. Here I want to draw a contrast between him and Gwynplaine from Victor Hugo's *The Man Who Laughs*. Both figures present a face of joy in the midst of deep pain. However, the latter, Gwynplaine, carries a cautionary tale for every parent.

While Guido's optimism and make-believe games are born out of love, aiming to shield his son from the brutal reality of their situation, Gwynplaine's disfigured, perpetual grin is a mask forced upon him. It stands not for genuine joy but for pain concealed and internalized. This mask, while making him a spectacle for many, hides a tumultuous storm of emotions: anguish, loneliness, and a desperate yearning for genuine connection and acceptance.

As parents preparing our children for an uncertain future, it's vital to understand the difference. There's a fine line between fostering real hope, optimism, and resilience, and merely painting on a happy face to hide genuine pain and despair. The former nurtures and empowers, while the latter can erode and mislead.

Being a Joyful Collapse Parent doesn't mean suppressing genuine feelings of fear, anxiety, or grief. It's not about pasting on a smile when your heart is heavy or feigning happiness when grappling with despair. Instead, it means acknowledging those feelings, addressing them, and guiding your children through them with authenticity. Our children, with their innate ability to sense emotions, will recognize a façade. And if they grow up believing that they must always hide their true feelings behind a smile, we risk teaching them to suppress their genuine emotions. This can lead to emotional dissonance, where they might feel compelled to project happiness while drowning in sorrow inside.

Resilience is built on authenticity, not denial. To prepare our children for the challenges ahead, we must equip them with the emotional intelligence to confront, understand, and navigate their feelings, not hide behind them. While it's essential to inject moments of levity, joy, and humor into our children's lives, let's ensure that these are born from a place of genuine love and understanding, not from a forced grin. Gwynplaine's story reminds us that the most potent smiles are those that resonate from within, unburdened by hidden pain.

3: Three Pillars of Holistic Education in Collapse

"Life is not measured by the number of breaths we take, but by the moments that take our breath away."

-Maya Angelou

Our relationship to our planet and ourselves is shifting, and the knowledge and skills we impart to the next generation will need to reflect this fundamental change. At this crossroads, there emerges a unique blend of the time-tested, the creative, and the introspective. By melding practical skills, creative endeavors, and intellectual pursuits, we can craft a robust, multifaceted education.

Practical Skills: A Return to Earth and Hand

Modern society, with its growing disconnect from nature and manual labor, often forgets the grounding sensation of hands in soil or the satisfaction of creating with raw materials. Practical skills like woodworking, farming, and general self-reliance offer more than just utility. They anchor us to the Earth, promoting a respect for nature, an understanding of the value of hard work, and the thrill of tangible results.

For example, when a child plants a seed, nurtures it, and sees it sprout, they witness the birth of life firsthand. When they craft something with their hands, they understand the importance of precision, patience, and perseverance. These skills lay a foundation for both self-sufficiency and a deep appreciation of the natural world around them.

Creativity: The Soul's Language

In our increasingly soulless capitalist existence, music, arts, and dance have often been relegated to extracurricular activities. But they are not that. They are the soul's language, the heartbeats of every civilization. Creativity, in its many forms, fosters emotional expression, encourages original thinking, and builds bridges across cultural and linguistic divides.

Children who engage in creative pursuits learn about themselves, their emotions, and the boundless ways they can communicate with themselves and those around them. From the rhythm of a dance to the brushstrokes on canvas, they discover avenues of expression that words will never capture. Moreover, creativity breeds resilience. The arts teach children that mistakes can be part of the process, that they can be sources of inspiration, and that there's always room for improvement and innovation.

Introspective Growth: The Intellectual Odyssey

While practical skills and creativity root us and allow us to express ourselves, introspective growth elevates our mind. Intellectual curiosity is above all a practice of cultivating a love for knowledge, understanding, and self-awareness. Encouraging children to question, to wonder, and to seek answers nurtures critical thinking and empathy.

Philosophers from Socrates to Confucius emphasized the importance of "knowing oneself." When children are pushed to reflect, challenge their beliefs, and develop their perspectives, they're not just gaining knowledge; they're evolving as thoughtful, conscious individuals. Remember, our brain is what separates us from other land animals. Our brains are so big that when you were a new parent, you had to hold your child's head up because it was too heavy. A newborn's skull has gaps in it because it has to collapse to get out of the birth canal. Our brains are massive, and the intellectual capacity within them reflects that.

Merging the Triad: The Holistic Individual

These three pillars—practical skills, creativity, and introspective growth—intertwine to form the wholesome individual. One who can fend for themselves yet understands the profound connection we share with others. One who can express, create, and understand the vast emotional spectrum of the human experience. And one who seeks, questions, and grows constantly, looking both outwards at their surroundings and inwards into themselves.

In this ever-changing landscape, it's not just about survival—it's about thriving. By instilling this trinity in the next generation, we're not just preparing them for a future of uncertainty but empowering them to shape it with joy, wisdom, and heart.

Practical Survival Skills: A Closer Look

At its core, the practical skills pillar emphasizes equipping our children with the tangible knowledge they'll need to navigate the complexities of a post-collapse environment. It encompasses a range of abilities from the basic to the advanced:

Basic Survival Skills: Understanding how to find and purify water, the knowledge to identify edible plants and herbs, and the ability to start a fire. These are foundational skills that will prove crucial in uncertain times.

Agricultural Know-how: As traditional food supply chains become unreliable, the ability to grow one's own food is invaluable. This involves understanding soil quality, crop rotation, natural pest control, and sustainable farming practices.

Handiwork and Repair: The "throwaway" culture might become a thing of the past. Repairing and reusing will be vital. Skills like sewing, mending, basic carpentry, and mechanics can make a significant difference in daily life.

First Aid and Health: Basic medical knowledge, from dressing wounds to understanding common ailments and their herbal remedies, will be pivotal in the absence of immediate medical facilities.

Community Building: Interpersonal skills, mediation, and community organization will be crucial as people come together to form new community structures or strengthen existing ones.

The Ancestral Connection: Honoring History Through Survival Skills

When we think of survival skills in our modern era, they often seem disconnected from our daily life, reserved for intrepid adventurers or post-apocalyptic scenarios. Yet, for the vast majority of human history, these skills were an essential part of living. Every day was a dance of survival, and every member of the community had their role in ensuring the collective thrived. By reconnecting with these basic survival abilities we grow two-fold: we acquire pragmatic tools and we embrace a legacy, forging an intimate link with our forebears.

Survival skills represent an accumulation of human wisdom, an anthology of trial and error, adaptation, and resilience. With every fire kindled, shelter constructed, or edible plant identified, we're tapping into thousands of years of shared human experience. It's a rich tapestry of stories, lessons, and memories passed down through countless generations. This connection to our ancestry bestows upon us a sense of purpose and grounding, reminding us that even in the face of immense challenges, we are part of a lineage that has thrived because of our perseverance.

Across diverse cultures, celebrating survival skills were often rites of passage, intricately woven into the fabric of societal norms and milestones. The Maasai of East Africa, for instance, have a deep-rooted warrior culture. Young Maasai boys embark on a journey into manhood, marked by a series of rituals and teachings. Among these is the ability to survive in the wild – understanding the terrain, knowing where to find water, and how to track animals. The culmination of this training is often a solitary excursion into the wilderness, where these skills are put to the test.

Indigenous American tribes, spread across diverse ecosystems, had a myriad of survival techniques tailored to their specific environments. Young members were taught hunting, fishing, foraging, and shelter-building as sacred duties that reflected their relationship with the land. This training was about more than survival; it was about understanding one's place in the greater web of life. Activities like vision quests, where adolescents would spend days alone in the wilderness seeking spiritual guidance and self-discovery, underscored the synthesis of survival and spirituality.

In the Australian Outback, the indigenous Aboriginal communities had a concept known as the "Walkabout." This rite of passage required young men to undertake a journey, lasting up to six months, where they lived off the land. This time of isolation, survival, and reflection was seen as a crucial period of growth, bridging the gap between boyhood and manhood.

These cultures and many others globally recognized the value of survival skills as more than just practical tools. They were avenues of personal development, gateways to spiritual growth, and a means to cement one's identity within the community. As we rekindle our relationship with these ancestral skills in our current context, we're doing more than preparing for possible challenges ahead. We're honoring our history, celebrating our shared human journey, and fostering a profound sense of continuity and belonging. This deep connection to our ancestors can serve as a backstop of strength as we navigate the uncharted terrains of uncertainty, knowing that resilience and adaptability is very deeply embedded in our DNA.

Practical Unity: Everyday Tasks and Their Survival Roots

These days, it's often easy to overlook the myriad ways our ancestors' survival skills continue to manifest in our modern routines. Practical unity is about recognizing and understanding the intimate bond between our current actions and the ancient wisdom that underpins them. These are not relics of a bygone era, they are living traditions that remind us of our shared human heritage.

Let's begin with something as ubiquitous as cooking. Every time we light our stoves, ovens, or barbecues, we're tapping into the ancient art of fire-making, an essential survival skill that allowed our ancestors to stay warm, fend off predators, and cook food. The action of lighting a fire, be it with matches or a lighter, is a modern manifestation of an age-old practice of creating friction or striking stones. The cooked meals we enjoy are a tribute to countless generations who learned the intricate dance of harvesting food and controlling the flame.

Consider the act of foraging when we walk through our local markets or grocery stores. While the surroundings are decidedly modern, the underlying skill of identifying beneficial foods and discerning them from potentially harmful ones echoes our forebears' knowledge. Every time we choose ripe fruits, fresh vegetables, or wholesome grains, we mirror the discernment of our ancestors who had to make these choices in wild settings, where a wrong pick could mean illness or worse.

Water collection is another elemental skill that manifests in our daily lives. When I turn on the tap, collect rainwater, or draw water from a well, I'm enacting a ritual as old as humanity itself. Our ancestors traveled great distances, sometimes migrating entirely, in pursuit of reliable water sources. They developed an innate understanding of water table patterns, understanding where to dig, and how deep to ensure a fresh supply. Every glass of water we drink is a nod to this ancient expertise.

Our modern homes, as varied and "smart" as they are, can trace their lineage back to the basic shelters of prehistory. Our ancestors were adept at reading the environment, choosing strategic locations that offered protection from elements and potential threats. Constructing shelters using available materials, from leaves and mud to snow and stone, was a crucial survival skill. Today, when we seek shade on a hot day or take refuge under an awning during rain, we are unconsciously echoing the instincts of our predecessors. Sure, it doesn't seem like much, after all you may just be protecting yourself with the simplest of shelters. But remember that there are no other living organisms that we know of that create the intricate kinds of shelters we do, and that is a result of generations upon generations of knowledge and practice.

And spare a thought for the humble knot. From tying shoelaces to securing loads on a vehicle, the art of knot-making and rope work is an integral part of many daily tasks. Our ancestors relied on this skill for various purposes, including setting traps, building structures, or crafting tools.

Embracing the philosophy of practical unity is about mindfulness. It's about pausing, even if for a moment, and acknowledging the deep-rooted connections between our modern actions and the survival skills that facilitated our journey as a species. Every routine task becomes a bridge to our shared history, a nod to the resilience, ingenuity, and adaptability that have always been hallmarks of the human experience. As we face the uncertainties of collapse, I find solace in knowing that our daily lives are intertwined with the time-tested wisdom of our ancestors.

Notable Resources for Survival Skills Education

***Bushcraft 101: A Field Guide to the Art of Wilderness Survival*, by Dave Canterbury**: This book offers practical advice on essential wilderness survival skills. Dave Canterbury, a survival expert, breaks down complex tasks into digestible lessons. It's a fantastic starting point, especially for those looking to introduce these skills to younger members of the family.

***The SAS Survival Handbook*, by John 'Lofty' Wiseman**: This comprehensive guide from a former SAS soldier covers everything from basic campcraft and navigation to strategies for coping with any type of disaster. It's detailed and extensive, making it a must-have reference for anyone serious about survival skills. Moreover, Wiseman's clear, instructive tone ensures that the knowledge is accessible to both adults and children.

Both these books, while grounded in practicality, do more than just teach skills. They instill a mindset of adaptability, resilience, and respect – qualities that will be invaluable as we navigate the challenges ahead. Indigenous and ancient tradition provides a rich understanding of survival skills and their connection to life and spirituality. Here are two notable works and authors that bridge this understanding.

***The Tracker* by Tom Brown Jr.**: Tom Brown Jr. is renowned for his knowledge of wilderness survival skills, which he learned from an Apache elder named Stalking Wolf when he was a child. "The Tracker" both delves into the author's experiences and teachings while elaborating on the deep connection between the land and its inhabitants. Brown's insights are not merely techniques, they're a philosophy, an understanding of what we see around us, derived from indigenous wisdom. His other works also delve into topics like awareness, philosophy, and tracking, and they all provide valuable lessons in survival and connectivity to nature.

***Sacred Plant Medicine: The Wisdom in Native American Herbalism* by Stephen Harrod Buhner**: In this profound exploration of the connections between the nature of plants and humans, Buhner dives deep into the indigenous practices of herbal medicine. Drawing from Native American traditions, this book illuminates the sacramental relationship between indigenous peoples and plants. Part herbal reference book, part guide, it delves into the spiritual and survival aspects of plant medicine, reminding readers of the profound connections our ancestors maintained with the natural world, recognizing plants as both resources and sentient beings with their wisdom and teachings.

Both these works emphasize not only the pragmatic aspects of survival but also the spiritual and philosophical underpinnings that ancient and indigenous cultures attached to these skills. They offer both techniques and a deeper appreciation for the life around us and our place within it.

Creativity and Art: The Soul's Language

Art, in its myriad forms, possesses a profound ability to evoke emotions, resonate with our innermost feelings, and transport us to places both familiar and fantastical. Deep within our humanity is this relentless pursuit of expression, even in the midst of deep disruption. For many, including myself, art isn't just a passive experience. It's a journey. A piece of artwork, whether it's a painting, a sculpture, a piece of music, or any other form, has the power to move us to tears, stir deep-rooted emotions, and awaken dormant feelings.

I am always moved by art that still exists long after the people that created them have passed. It can feel like having a direct connection with these ancient people, seeing and feeling what they saw and felt way back when. The ancient rock art of Murujuga is a unique example of human expression and creativity. Located on what is today the Burrup Peninsula of Western Australia, this ancient canvas tells stories that have withstood millenia, illustrating the eternal power of human expression to convey, connect, and cope. There is a sublime imagery as well, rock holding firm and art still visible in a time that looks nothing like the world the artist knew.

The lasting artistry of Murujuga offers a fundamental reminder–it emphasizes the profound role creativity plays in helping societies endure hardships, find purpose, and foster connection. These ageless carvings, bearing images of ancient rituals, celestial events, and the delicate dance of life, highlight our deep-seated need to express, to be heard, and to leave a lasting imprint. They remind us that in the darkest times, our inherent creativity becomes a source of comfort and a tool for resilience.

The Lascaux Caves in southwestern France stand as silent witnesses to another of humanity's earliest known artistic endeavors. Within these subterranean chambers lie intricate paintings of animals and symbolic graphics, believed to be over 17,000 years old. These ancient artists, with rudimentary tools and a limited palette, showcased a profound understanding of movement and perspective, capturing the essence of the animals with stunning accuracy. More than mere depictions, these paintings are believed to have held spiritual significance, possibly related to rituals or star constellations. In the flickering torchlight, these ancient images come alive, dancing and prancing on the cave walls, narrating tales of a time long gone, yet palpably present.

Several millennia later, but with an equally powerful artistic spirit, the caves of Ajanta and Ellora in India stand as monuments to the prowess and vision of ancient Indian artisans. Carved into the rocky Deccan plateau, these caves house a plethora of sculptures and murals, each more exquisite than the last. The Ajanta Caves, primarily Buddhist, are adorned with intricate paintings narrating the Jataka tales – stories of Buddha's former births. The Ellora caves, showcasing the artistic zenith reached by Buddhist, Hindu, and Jain artisans, are a confluence of religious harmony. Their art is both an illustration of faith and an immersive experience of divinity, detailing our created narratives of gods, goddesses, and legendary heroes.

While both these examples offer an incredible look into the way art can anchor a larger social context, art can also provide individuals a way to release emotions and pain in beautiful ways, and we have had so many artistic lights that capture that spirit.

One such light was Frida Kahlo, a name synonymous with unabashed self-expression. Born in Mexico, Kahlo's daily life was an almost impossible crucible of physical and emotional pain, but it was also one of fierce determination and groundbreaking creativity. Her art was her sanctuary, a refuge where she bared her soul, unafraid and unapologetic. Kahlo's paintings, often self-portraits, were windows into her soul, reflecting her pain, love, anguish, and revolutionary spirit. In a space dominated by male artists, Kahlo broke the mold, not just with her art but with her unbreakable soul, paving the way for countless female artists after her. I've been to her home in Coyocán many times, and there you can feel the palpable tension between the prison that was her body, and the freedom that was her art.

The power of art lies in both its aesthetic appeal and in its ability to communicate, to resonate, and to inspire. In the brushstrokes of the Lascaux cave painters, the chisel marks of the Ajanta and Ellora artisans, and the vivid palette of Frida Kahlo, we find echoes of shared human experiences — love, loss, pain, despair, and, most importantly, joy.

Why does art hold such sway over our emotions? Perhaps because it is a borderless manifestation of our internal selves. Art transcends linguistic, cultural, and temporal barriers, reaching out and touching souls across time and space. A haunting melody, a poignant sculpture, or a riveting painting resonates with our souls, evoking emotions that often lie buried beneath the weight of daily existence.

And today, and into our kids' futures, the importance of art becomes even more pronounced. Art offers solace in times of despair, and a source of inspiration to reframe the outside world. It reminds us of the beauty that exists everywhere, of our boundless creativity, and of the unbreakable humanity that is threaded through all of us.

Guiding the Next Generation through the Sanctuary of Creativity

In times of upheaval and uncertainty, as parents, we often grapple with the challenge of sheltering our children, trying to offer them a semblance of stability. However, if history and the examples above have taught us anything, art and creativity isn't simply a form of escape, but a lifeline, a way to process, understand, and transcend our current reality.

Art and creativity can provide our children a channel to express their fears, anxieties, and dreams. When words falter and emotions overwhelm, a canvas, a piece of clay, or the strings of a musical instrument can offer a simple and ancient medium for catharsis and comprehension. By encouraging our young ones to delve into the world of art, we give them a sanctuary, a space where they can be unapologetically themselves, navigating their internal landscapes and mirroring it onto tangible, creative expression.

Moreover, the act of creation fosters a sense of continuity. It becomes a bridge between the past, present, and future, anchoring them to the age-old traditions of our ancestors while equipping them with tools to envision and shape a better tomorrow. As guardians of the next generation, it's incumbent upon us to inspire and nurture their artistic inclinations. We must facilitate spaces of uninhibited expression, provide resources, and, most importantly, be present, celebrating each stroke, note, or craft they produce. In the shadow of our current moment, illuminating our children's paths with the radiant glow of creativity is more crucial than ever. For in this journey, art isn't just a pastime; it's a compass, guiding them toward resilience and a deeper understanding of their own life, and the lives around them.

Frida Kahlo, and many before her, taught us the profound power of transmuting pain into creation. Living through immense physical agony and emotional turbulence, she used her canvas as an outlet for her deepest vulnerabilities and most raw emotions. In our current moment, where feelings of despair and impotency loom for the upcoming generations, Frida's artistry serves as an example of reclaiming our own agency.

It reminds parents and caregivers that fostering creative expression in children can provide them with a potent tool to navigate their anguish and fears. As they grapple with a planet that may often seem beyond repair, just as Frida translated her struggles onto vibrant canvases, our children too can channel their feelings through myriad art forms. This not only helps them process and understand their emotions but also builds resilience and inner peace. For in the act of creation, even in the darkest moments, there is an inherent affirmation of the best of our humanity.

Introspective Growth: The Intellectual Odyssey

"There is nothing noble in being superior to some other man. The true nobility is in being superior to your previous self." -Mahatma Gandhi

As we move into our kids' futures, external markers of success, power dynamics, and traditional hierarchies can and will be upended overnight at times. Mahatma Gandhi offers us a useful compass for finding strength and meaning, and underscores the essence of introspective growth and its immense value, especially in times of societal collapse and restructuring.

Introspection, at its core, is a journey inwards. While everything around us may be chaotic and unpredictable, the inner landscape of our thoughts, feelings, and beliefs offers a sanctuary, a place where growth is possible despite external constraints. In an age where external markers may lose significance, the only real metric that remains is how much one has evolved in understanding, wisdom, and self-awareness. This inward journey is not about narcissistic self-focus but about truly understanding oneself, accepting our flaws, and working towards becoming better.

Gandhi's life epitomized this philosophy. Amidst the colossal challenges of colonial rule and the immense task of galvanizing a diverse and vast country like India towards its freedom, he frequently turned inwards. His experiments with truth were deeply personal endeavors to refine his own character, beliefs, and actions. He sought not to be superior to others but to his past self, and this allowed him to navigate the difficult waters of political and societal upheaval with some modicum of grace and fortitude.

In the context of our societal upheaval, introspective growth assumes an even greater importance. The external might be uncertain, presenting challenges that seem insurmountable. In such scenarios, drawing comparisons with others can lead to feelings of despair, envy, or superiority—all of which are counterproductive. The only comparison that truly matters is one that is internal. Have we become more resilient, understanding, and wise? Have we learned to navigate challenges with more grace, patience, and innovation?

For the future generations, this introspective growth will be an essential tool for survival and well-being. The challenges they'll face will be unprecedented, and external comparisons, deciding your worth based on what others think, may lead to disillusionment. The emphasis should not be on outdoing others but on outgrowing one's own limitations, fears, and biases. Every day presents an opportunity to evolve, and our human mind is great at that.

This introspective journey will also be vital for emotional and psychological health. In a society undergoing unprecedented change, mental well-being will be as crucial as physical survival. By focusing on personal growth and self-improvement, individuals can find purpose, meaning, and a sense of achievement even in the direst circumstances. Such an approach also fosters community and collaboration. When each individual is focused on personal growth rather than external superiority, the collective mindset shifts from competition to cooperation.

For parents preparing their children for such a future, the emphasis should be on cultivating introspective habits from a young age. Encourage children to reflect on their actions, understand their emotions, and strive for personal growth. Equip them with tools like journaling, meditation, and thoughtful reading that propel introspective thinking. Teach them to celebrate personal milestones and view mistakes as opportunities for growth.

Merging the Triad: Cultivating a Holistic Path to Self-Preservation

As we live in the midst of this profound transformation, equipping the next generation to navigate the challenges of collapse necessitates a broad and interconnected approach. "Practical Survival Skills", "Creativity and Art", and "Introspective Growth" come together to form a triad, each component reinforcing and elevating the others. The true potency of this triad is realized when they are seamlessly interwoven in the daily lives of our children, ensuring they possess not only the means to survive but to thrive and find meaning amidst upheaval. I can imagine myself nurturing these aspects in my child's life:

Practical Survival Skills: Weekends spent camping can evolve into lessons about shelter-building or foraging. Everyday tasks, like mending a torn garment or preserving food, become hands-on training. Families might gather around to listen to a grandparent's stories, hearing about past experiences, and understanding the ancestral wisdom inherent in our daily survival. As children learn these skills that will help them sustain themselves, they're also connecting with the lineage of humanity, understanding the resilience and resourcefulness that have always been at our core.

Creativity and Art: In the evenings, after dinner, the family might gather around for storytelling sessions, each member, young and old, contributing a piece, preserving memories while fostering imagination. Walls of their home turn into canvases as children paint their dreams and their fears, echoing the spirit of ancient ancestors who created the works of Lascaux or Murujuga. A visit to a local museum or art exhibition goes beyond being a recreational outing, it becomes a chance to appreciate humanity's collective soul and the transcendent power of art. Perhaps there's a corner in their home with a guitar or a keyboard, where impromptu musical sessions ignite song and dance.

Introspective Growth: The parent encourages dialogue, fostering an environment where questions are celebrated. Dinner discussions might revolve around philosophical dilemmas, echoing the Socratic method, pushing boundaries of thought. The child learns early on the value of reflection, perhaps maintaining a journal or practicing meditation. They're taught the power of personal growth, often drawing inspiration from global figures like Gandhi. Through introspective exercises, they gradually build a robust internal compass, one that will guide them when external landmarks fade.

As parents weave these pillars into their child's upbringing, they're essentially crafting a holistic armor. The triad not only ensures that children are well-equipped to face practical challenges but are also emotionally and intellectually fortified.

They learn to value the deep wellsprings of creativity that can offer solace and expression in difficult times and understand the importance of continuous self-evolution. But even more than survival tools, I think this triad also serves as a foundation for self-preservation. In a world of uncertainties, they provide a roadmap, a reminder that even in the face of the future, we can persevere, innovate, and grow. By emphasizing these three pillars, parents are not just preparing their children for collapse; they're equipping them with the tools to rebuild, reimagine, and reclaim the future.

4: **Fun with Collapse: Embrace Life's Little Joys**

"What can you do to promote world peace? Go home and love your family."

-Mother Teresa

In this chapter, I want to offer some concrete actions that you as a parent can begin today. We're of course, poised on the precipice of the unprecedented, yet, it is precisely in these times that we must remember a fundamental truth of human existence: joy is not just found in grand triumphs or life-altering revelations; it is often nestled in the simplest, most unassuming moments.

"Fun with Collapse," is not about diminishing the seriousness of our predicament, but about offering a different lens. It's a call to action, urging us to turn our attention to the variety of tiny pleasures and small moments of light that life gives us. There's a certain audacity in claiming joy in the midst of collapse, and there's power too—a resilience that comes from finding laughter amidst tears, warmth in the coldest nights, and beauty in the midst of chaos.

But why now, you might wonder? Because collapse isn't a far-off event looming on the horizon; its signs are inching into our lives in real-time. Every day, we face small reminders of the change around us, from unpredictable weather patterns to shifting social dynamics. Waiting for a cataclysmic moment to begin seeking joy will leave us unprepared and overwhelmed.

Instead, I hope we can adopt a proactive approach. Let's dive into a series of activities designed for both preparation and celebration. These are actionable, concrete steps aimed at weaving joy, laughter, and lightness of spirit into the fabric of our daily lives. They challenge us to reexamine our values, our routines, and our expectations. In doing so, we might discover that while the grand spectacles of life have their allure, the true essence of living can be found in the small, seemingly mundane moments that bring genuine happiness.

To embark on this journey of 'Fun with Collapse' is to declare that, even as we prepare for the challenges ahead, we will not let the weight of the world snuff out our joy. Because if there's one thing more contagious than despair, it's the infectious spark of laughter that can light up even our darkest corners. And remember, every journey starts with a single step, or in our case, with a smile and a heart filled with lightness. Let's start now. The future may be uncertain, but our capacity for joy remains firmly within our own agency.

My Stockpile of Cinnamon Toast Crunch

As the reality of potential societal collapse loomed ever closer, I found myself pouring over lists of essential goods to stockpile. From bottled water to first aid kits, the catalog of "essentials" seemed endless. Each item was practical, necessary, but coldly impersonal. They were the sustenance of survival, not the food of the soul.

One evening, when I was perusing the aisles at Grocery Outlet, a memory washed over me like milk washing over a bowl of cereal. I was a child again, in pajamas, watching Saturday morning cartoons with a bowl of Cinnamon Toast Crunch. Each bite, a hammer blow of sugary heaven, represented the pure joy and wide eyed mornings of childhood.

A revelation struck me. What was the point of preparing for a future if it was devoid of joy? So, amidst bewildered glances from other shoppers, I filled my cart with boxes of Cinnamon Toast Crunch. Every single one they had on the shelves. To them, it might have seemed frivolous. But to me, it was a declaration: today, and from now on, I would stockpile not just for survival, but for joy, cherishing those moments that make life truly worth living.

Activity: Create Your Joyful Collapse Grocery List

Purpose: To identify and stockpile non-perishable foods that not only provide sustenance but also bring immense joy and remind you of cherished memories.

Materials:

- ☐ Pen & paper or a digital device for note-taking
- ☐ Personal memories
- ☐ A sense of adventure

Steps:

1. Memory Lane Stroll: Begin by closing your eyes and reminiscing about your favorite food-related memories. Did you have a favorite snack after school? A guilty pleasure that you would sneak into your room? A comfort food that made rainy days better?

2. List Down the Joyful Foods: On your paper or device, start listing these foods. Don't think about their nutritional value or if they are "practical." This is about joy, not just sustenance.

3. The Can-Can Dance: Explore your current pantry or your local store. Look specifically for the non-perishable versions of your joyful foods. For instance, if you loved fresh peaches as a kid, maybe there's a canned version that still brings that zest. Adore chocolate? Look for long-lasting chocolate syrups or cocoa powder.

4. Expand Your Horizon: While personal memories are a great starting point, be open to discovering new sources of joy. Maybe you've never tried Spam or Vienna sausages, but now could be the time to give them a shot. Be curious!

5. Organize and Store: Once you have a list, figure out storage. Remember, while some items like canned goods have a longer shelf life, others might need rotation to stay fresh. Create a system that allows you to consume and replenish these joy-bringers.

6. Share and Celebrate: Engage with family members or close friends in this activity. What's on their Joyful Collapse Grocery List? Sharing can lead to delightful discoveries. Maybe your best friend's favorite is a cereal you've never tried, or your sibling swears by a particular brand of canned soup.

Every time you dive into your joyful stockpile, let it be a reminder that preparing for uncertain times is not just about surviving, but also about living – about cherishing moments of delight amidst the chaos. After all, the essence of joyful collapse parenting lies not just in protection, but in celebration.

And remember, you're not necessarily saving all of your stockpile for some unknown time in the future. While your grocery store still has a stock of your favorite joyful foods, you can break into your stash whenever you want. Just have a little fun with it.

Keeping Memories Accessible: Get Your Nostalgia Together

In an era dominated by digital connections and cloud storage, our most cherished memories—photos, videos, written snippets—are often floating somewhere in virtual space. Yet, as we navigate potential future uncertainties, there's undeniable value in reclaiming these memories from the ether. Having offline access ensures that regardless of internet connectivity, technological changes, or unforeseen disruptions, our treasured moments remain close. They serve as an enduring encapsulation of our stories, grounding us in our history while providing solace and joy in moments of introspection, and most crucially, they stand resilient against the vulnerabilities of the online world.

Activity: Crafting Your Memory Vault

Purpose: To create an offline, tangible archive of your memories that can be accessed, shared, and cherished without relying on online cloud services. In times of uncertainty, these memories provide a source of comfort, grounding, and a reminder of life's joys.

Materials:

- ☐ USB drives or external hard drives
- ☐ Burnable CDs or DVDs (optional but recommended)
- ☐ CD/DVD-ROM (optional but recommended)
- ☐ Photo-printing service
- ☐ Durable photo album or memory box
- ☐ Solar-powered charger or backup battery
- ☐ Computer or device for viewing and sorting

Steps:

1. Digital Declutter: Start by accessing your cloud services. Browse through your photos and videos, selecting only the most significant and meaningful moments. It's a time to focus on quality, not quantity.

2. Transfer to Offline Storage: Download your chosen memories.

For digital memories: Transfer them to your USB drives or external hard drives. For added backup, I would recommend burning them onto CDs or DVDs, as they won't be affected by possible high-intensity EM pulses.

For physical copies: Use a photo-printing service to print your cherished photos and store them in your photo album or memory box.

Prepare for Power-Outs: If you're relying on digital memories, ensure you have a solar-powered charger or backup battery pack. This makes sure you can view your memories even during power outages.

3. Display and Share: If you've opted for physical photos, consider creating a photo wall or memory board in your living space.

4. Create a Tradition: For digital memories, set a tradition. Maybe a "memories night" where you gather to watch old videos with your family.

5. Regular Refresh: Every few months, revisit your memory vault. Add new memories, check the condition of storage devices, and refresh your content. It's an opportunity to reconnect with your past and ensure your vault stays updated.

Closing Thought: Your memories are a testament to your journey, the highs and the lows, the everyday moments, and the milestones. By preserving them offline, you ensure that they remain accessible, no matter what the future holds, grounding you in love, laughter, and life's shared experiences.

The Power of Cinema: A Portal to Imagination for Families

"In the hands of a great filmmaker, the world of cinema can be a shared dream," Steven Spielberg once remarked. Indeed, the power of film and television transcends mere entertainment. For families, especially in challenging times like collapse, these shared narratives provide a unique respite—a portal that transports us to realms unbounded by our current reality. While we deal with the unending uncertainty of our time, these shared cinematic experiences offer solace and connection.

Legendary director Martin Scorsese captured this sentiment when he said, "Movies touch our hearts and awaken our vision, and change the way we see things." It's a truth any family can attest to when cuddling together on a couch, immersed in a story that ignites laughter, tears, and spirited discussions. During such moments, the walls of our living room dissolve, and we are momentarily free, journeying to distant lands or even galaxies.

In the face of collapse, the imagination becomes a sanctuary. It's in these shared visions, in the glow of the screen, that families can find both an escape and a binding thread—a reminder that even in adversity, we can dream, we can hope, and we can journey together.

The Impermanence of Digital Clouds

In our modern age, the ethereal 'cloud' has become a vault for our cherished memories and favorite films. With a simple click, a universe of stories is at our fingertips. But like a mirage, this digital oasis can be gone in an instant. As we come to grips with the reality of collapse, the fragility of our online repositories becomes starkly evident. In an era where streaming has replaced physical media, and digital libraries have replaced DVD shelves, we must pause and ponder: What if the cloud dissipates? What if, amidst infrastructural challenges or the general side effects of living in a hellscape, we lose access to these digital troves?

Losing these narratives—these shared memories—is about the shared experiences, the lessons learned, and the countless hours families have bonded over these stories. It underscores the importance of ensuring that our beloved movies and shows, those that have the power to uplift our spirits and transport us to any place we want, remain accessible, even when the digital realm becomes unreachable.

For families preparing for the uncertainties ahead, it's imperative to think about preserving these shared moments. Just as we would safeguard family photos or heirloom recipes, so too must we consider the value of the films and shows that have shaped our familial bonds.

Activity: Crafting Your Cinematic Vault

Purpose:
In uncertain times, cinema provides an escape, a unifying experience, and a source of inspiration. This activity ensures

that you and your family can continue enjoying your favorite films and TV shows, even if digital access becomes compromised.

Materials:

- [ ] A list of your family's all-time favorite films and TV shows.
- [ ] DVD/Blu-ray player or a projector system (ensure it can function without continuous internet access).
- [ ] DVD/Blu-ray copies of your favorite movies and shows.
- [ ] Storage case or shelving for the physical copies.
- [ ] Optional: A backup power source, like a portable generator or solar charger.

Steps:

1. Gathering Favorites: Sit down with your family and make a list of must-have movies and TV shows. Think of those films that never get old, ones that elicit laughter, tears, or profound thinking every time.

2. Physical Acquisition: Start acquiring physical copies of these favorites. Look into stores that sell DVDs and Blu-rays, or even check local thrift shops, garage sales, or online marketplaces.

3. Storage: Dedicate a space in your home as your 'Cinematic Vault'. Organize your collection in a manner that's easy to navigate. You might categorize by genre, director, or family member's favorites.

4. Regular Movie Nights: Introduce or continue the tradition of family movie nights. This ensures you're making use of your collection and provides regular bonding time.

5. Backup Power: In the event of power disruptions, having a backup power option ensures your movie nights remain uninterrupted. If you've invested in a backup power solution for other purposes, test it with your entertainment system to ensure compatibility.

6. Expand the Vault: As you come across more films or shows that resonate with your family, keep adding them to your collection.

Remember, the magic of cinema lies in both the stories on screen and in the shared experience of watching them together. This vault isn't just a collection of disks; it's a reservoir of shared memories, emotions, and lessons. No matter what is happening outside our homes, these stories remain a reminder of the incredible ability we have to create beautiful, funny, and thought provoking visual storytelling.

Connection Through the Ancient Art of Oral Storytelling

In many traditional societies, the art of storytelling was intrinsically linked with leadership. Take the Griots of the Mande cultures in West Africa, for instance. These were both skilled musicians and master storytellers. The mantle of leadership within the community was often associated with one's ability to weave captivating narratives.

The Griot's narratives were more than simple entertainment; they were the living chronicles of their people. These tales encapsulated history, moral lessons, traditions, and the collective memory of the community. The Griot's gift was in making the past come alive, making listeners feel connected to their ancestors and traditions, often so deeply that listeners felt their ancestors were truly sitting amongst them.

For the Mande people, the Griot was a storyteller, a historian, advisor, praise singer, and mediator. Their ability to engage an audience, invoke emotion, and impart wisdom was seen as a potent skill. Through their stories, Griots preserved the societal fabric, passed down values, and ensured that the community's heritage continued from one generation to the next. This rich tradition underscores the profound respect many ancient cultures had for the confluence of leadership and storytelling.

Through their stories, these leaders maintained societal cohesion, instilled moral values, and ensured the continuity of traditions. It was a celebration of the deep-rooted belief in many ancient cultures that the best leaders were first dream-weavers and storytellers, connecting the past, present, and future through the magic of their words.

Activity: Crafting Your Oral Storytelling Kit

Purpose:
To reconnect with the ancient art of oral storytelling and ensure that families can access and share these treasured tales, passing down wisdom, joy, and lessons of life.

Materials:

- ☐ A notebook or journal
- ☐ Colored pens or pencils
- ☐ Small tokens or trinkets (these can be everyday objects that hold significance, like a feather, a coin, or a dried flower)
- ☐ A small box or pouch to store the tokens

Steps:

1. Family Discussion: Start by gathering as a family and discussing favorite stories or family memories. These could be folktales, family anecdotes, or even imaginative tales.

2. Token Selection: For each story, select a token that represents it. For example, a feather might remind you of a tale about a bird's adventure, or a coin might symbolize a story about an ancestor's journey to a new land.

3. Journaling: In the notebook, dedicate a page to each token. Write down the name of the story the token represents and a few keywords or a short summary. Over time, this will help jog your memory and set the stage for the storytelling.

4. Storytelling Sessions: Regularly set aside time for 'Oral Storytelling Sessions'. A family member picks a token from the box without looking, and the storyteller uses the token as a cue to share that particular tale. Rotate the storyteller role among family members.

5. Add to the Kit: As you encounter new stories or remember forgotten ones, add new tokens to your kit. Encourage children to come up with their stories and select a token for them.

6. Share and Listen: The beauty of oral storytelling lies not just in the telling but in the listening. Encourage active listening, ask questions, and immerse in the narrative fully. This shared experience will fortify family bonds and preserve stories for generations to come.

Remember, the aim is not perfection but connection. Embrace the unique flavors each family member brings to their storytelling, and watch as this ancient practice brings warmth, joy, and a sense of rootedness to your family.

Harmony Amidst Collapse: The Effusive Energy of Music and Dance

When the world gets tough, the comforting notes of a familiar song can transport us to moments of past joy, grounding us in memories that can make us smile or bring a happy tear to our eye. Music becomes a balm, quieting internal unrest and reminding us of our collective enduring spirit.

Creating music amidst collapse holds its own unique power. Playing an instrument isn't a diversion— in fact it's an act of defiance, a statement that even in the face of unthinkable chaos, we can find our own calming harmonies. Each chord struck or melody sung moves us, and shows us our capacity to innovate and adapt, transforming despair into art and uncertainty into creative expression.

Dance, too, emerges as a powerful response to the encroaching darkness. With each step and twirl, we embrace the present, converting anxiety into motion and trepidation into choreographed elegance. It's a raw, unfiltered celebration of the moment, an embodiment of our incredible ability to find pockets of joy amidst the chaos.

As we journey deeper into this era of collapse, let's not just preserve, but further amplify the role of music and dance in our lives. Let music serve as reminders of the beauty that persists, the communities that endure, and the spirit that, no matter the external discord, continues to craft melodies of passion and resilience.

Activity: Crafting Melodies of Togetherness (for those who do not play an instrument)

Purpose:
To familiarize oneself with a musical instrument that's beginner-friendly and set the stage for heartfelt family sing-alongs, strengthening bonds and creating lasting memories amidst challenging times.

Materials:

- ☐ A beginner-friendly musical instrument such as the ukulele, mandolin, kalimba, or harmonica.
- ☐ Basic instruction books or tutorials tailored for your chosen instrument (there are countless online resources

available, but it might be wise to print or purchase physical ones for continued access).

- ☐ A metronome (or a metronome app) to assist with rhythm.
- ☐ A selection of simple, well-known songs with chords and lyrics. Think about timeless classics or favorite family tunes.

Steps:

1. Choosing the Right Instrument: Start with the instrument that appeals to you the most. Consider size, sound, and portability. The ukulele, for instance, is lightweight and has a cheerful sound, while the harmonica is ultra-portable and versatile.

2. Begin with Basics: Dedicate the first few sessions to understanding the parts of the instrument, its tuning, and the correct way to hold and play it.

3. Practice Regularly: Set aside dedicated time daily or weekly for practice. Start with basic scales to get a feel for the instrument and gradually move to simple songs as you grow more comfortable.

4. Introduce Sing-alongs: Once you've mastered a few chords and can strum smoothly, gather your family, and introduce them to the joy of singing along. Choose songs that are well-loved and known by most, if not all, family members.

5. Encourage Family Participation: If other family members show interest, consider getting them their instruments or even percussion instruments like tambourines or shakers to join in the fun.

6. Expand Your Repertoire: As you progress, keep adding new songs to your list. Encourage family members to suggest songs they'd like to sing.

7. Celebrate Small Wins: Every new chord learned or song played is a milestone. Celebrate these moments and share the joy and achievement with your family.

Remember, the objective isn't to become a virtuoso but to find a new medium through which to connect, share, and find joy with your loved ones. Music, in its simplicity, offers comfort and cohesion, reminding us of the threads that bind us in song and melody.

The Power of Gardening

"Life begins the day you start a garden." - Japanese Proverb

In these mind-bending times, there's a profound solace found in the simple act of planting a seed and watching it grow. Gardening becomes a visible reminder of life's resilience, a true grounding in an environment overshadowed by degradation. Amidst the chaos around us, the rhythmic and patient nature of gardening grounds us, reminding us of where we come from, and the soil and leaves that allow us our breath.

By nurturing the soil and tending to plants families will foster a bond with the Earth and also with one another. The garden, in this context, becomes a haven—a living, breathing space where each member, regardless of age, contributes, learns, and marvels at the magic of life's persistence.

While societal structures may crumble and familiar landscapes alter, the sun will continue to rise, and plants will seek its warmth. Every bud that blooms and every fruit that ripens stands as a tangible example of nature's lesson in perseverance. Gardening, especially during collapse, allows us to produce food and beautifying spaces while standing as a defiant and joyous act of affirming life, and of seeing growth amidst decline. We may not be able to fully understand what's happening around us, but we can draw strength from our garden—a space where life begins fresh, every single day.

Activity: Crafting Your Family Garden Vault

Purpose:
To cultivate a resilient space that fosters family togetherness, joy, and the wonder of nurturing life, whether through edible produce or the simple beauty of nature's blossoms.

Materials:

- [ ] Seed packets (select a variety of your favorite flowers, vegetables, and herbs).
- [ ] Airtight containers or a seed storage box for storing seeds.
- [ ] Small pots or garden beds, depending on available space.
- [ ] Organic soil and compost.
- [ ] Watering cans or hose.
- [ ] Gardening tools like trowels, gloves, and pruners.
- [ ] Garden markers or labels.

☐ A journal or notebook to document the garden's journey.

Steps:

1. **Research and Select**: Begin by understanding your local climate and soil type. This will guide which seeds are best suited for your garden. Include a mix of plants for beauty and sustenance. Remember, even if you're gardening just for joy, the sight of a sunflower or the scent of lavender can be as nourishing as any vegetable.

2. **Seed Collection**: Purchase seeds from reliable sources, ensuring they are non-GMO and preferably organic. Store them in a cool, dry place, using airtight containers. Label them clearly with the name and planting instructions.

3. **Garden Spot**: Decide on a gardening space. This could be pots on a balcony, a backyard garden bed, or even a community garden plot. Ensure the location gets adequate sunlight and has good soil.

4. **Soil Prep**: Prepare the soil by loosening it with gardening tools and enriching it with compost. This will provide a fertile foundation for your seeds.

5. **Planting Time**: Following the instructions on the seed packets, plant your seeds at the recommended depth. Use garden markers to label each section or pot.

6. **Family Ritual**: Make planting a family event. Assign roles—someone to dig, someone to plant, someone to water. Share stories for each plant as you lay its seed into the ground.

7. Document the Journey: Use the journal to note down when you planted each seed, when they germinated, and any other observations. This can be a delightful way for kids to practice observation and patience.

8. Regular Care: Water, weed, and watch! Make tending to the garden a daily family activity. Celebrate each sprout, each bud, and every harvest, no matter how small.

9. Harvest and Enjoy: Once your plants bear fruit or bloom, celebrate the harvest. Prepare a meal using the vegetables or arrange the flowers in a vase for everyone to admire.

10. Reflect and Prepare for Next Season: At the end of each season, reflect on the journey. What did you learn? Which plants thrived, and which struggled? Save seeds from your plants for the next season and expand your garden vault.

Remember, the joy lies not just in the blooming flowers or the harvested vegetables but in the shared moments of togetherness, learning, and growth that the garden nurtures within the family. Though growing your own tasty squash stew isn't too bad either.

Collecting Your Favorite Jokes

"The most wasted of all days is one without laughter."

-E.E. Cummings

This quote cuts deep, especially in tumultuous times when uncertainty seems to be the only constant. Laughter, that spontaneous eruption of joy, serves as a powerful antidote to all the heaviness that surrounds us, offering a way out of our overwhelmed minds.

Laughter alleviates our burdens, even if for no more than a hot second, and fortifies our spirit, enabling us to confront challenges head-on. The humor encapsulated in jokes provides a shared experience, a burst of communal joy that binds us, creating a profound sense of belonging and unity. Every culture, every civilization, boasts its treasury of jokes that captures its essence, its worldview, and its core.

In the backdrop of the impending death spiral, this age-old tradition of sharing jokes gains even greater significance. These light-hearted narratives remind us of our shared humanity, our collective perseverance, and our indomitable spirit. They stand as defiant challenges to despair, like opening a curtain to bring light into a dark room.

As we navigate this unprecedented chapter in our lives, let's treasure the power of a good joke, the warmth of shared laughter. Within these moments of pure, unbridled joy, we might even find something more sublime within us, something to walk with us through this ridiculous time and place.

Activity: Build your Jokes Repository

Purpose:
To instill a sense of humor, provide a go-to source for light-hearted moments, and ensure that the art of joke-telling doesn't get lost in the hustle of life. Humor has a way of breaking barriers, providing relief during tense moments, and fostering connections. This repository isn't just a collection of jokes, but an archive of laughter and shared memories.

Materials:

- ☐ A few large joke books (e.g., "1000 Dumb Jokes" and similar titles).
- ☐ A dedicated notebook or digital document for personal and family favorite jokes.
- ☐ Pens, markers, or digital devices (depending on your preference for recording).
- ☐ A sense of humor

Steps:

1. Start with Personal Favorites: Begin by asking each family member to recall and record their all-time favorite jokes. Everyone has a joke or two that always gets them giggling or has special sentimental value.

2. Dive into the Joke Books: Instead of reading them cover-to-cover, randomly flip to a page and read a joke. This spontaneous selection ensures that even the reader is delighted and surprised. Over time, as you come across real gems, jot them down in your personal jokes notebook or digital document.

3. Categorize if Desired: Just as you might with a photo album, you can categorize jokes – dad jokes, knock-knock jokes, holiday-themed groaners, etc. This makes it fun when you're in the mood for a specific type of humor.

4. Share and Grow: Whenever family or friends gather, make it a tradition to share a new joke from the repository. Encourage guests to contribute their favorite jokes too.

5. Revisit and Refresh: Just like any archive, it's essential to revisit and refresh the content. Maybe every month, or during family gatherings, set aside some time to go through the repository, adding new jokes and reminiscing over the old ones.

Remember: The primary goal isn't to have the most extensive collection but to foster connections, create shared moments of joy, and ensure that the delightful art of joke-telling remains alive in your family's heart. Don't rush through the books; savor the unexpected chuckles and the eye-rolling puns. And most importantly, let laughter fill your lungs until it comes out of your nostrils.

Charting Your Own Path to Joy

The journey through this chapter has taken us through a variety of activities that can light up our days with happiness, grounding, and meaningful connection, especially in the face of an uncertain future. However, the activities I've outlined are by no means exhaustive. The real essence is in building a sustainable practice with your children around anything that holds deep meaning and joy for you and them.

The night sky, for instance, is a carpet of wonder and imagination. Stargazing can transport you to the vastness of the universe, reminding you of the grand scale of things and the transient beauty of our own existence. The act of cooking or baking, where raw ingredients transform into delicious outcomes, can be both a lesson in science and an exercise in creativity. Board games are not just about winning or losing; they teach strategy, patience, and the beauty of playful competition. And there's an indescribable satisfaction in crafting or building something with your own hands, be it a piece of art, a piece of furniture, or a tiny model.

Ultimately, it's essential to remember that joy doesn't lie solely in the activity itself but in the shared experience, the laughter, the conversations, and the memories you create. As we navigate the complexities and uncertainties of the present, let's find solace and strength in life's little joys, teaching our children the power of resilience, compassion, and happiness. Your journey of joy is unique to you; craft it, nurture it, love it.

5: Humor as Resistance and Release

"Like a welcome summer rain, humor may suddenly cleanse and cool the earth, the air, and you."

-Langston Hughes

There isn't a time in history where humor hasn't stood as a pillar of humanity, holding us up even during the most complicated times. A laugh, a grin, a smirk—they've been our defense mechanisms, our silent protests, and at times, our subversive weapons. The very act of laughing in the face of hardship demonstrates our resilience, and it's a mode of passive resistance, a defiance against the oppressors and the looming darkness.

Humor, in many historical contexts, has been a tool to blunt the force of aggressors. Those in power often utilize fear as their most potent weapon, but what fear fails to grasp is that it becomes impotent in the face of mockery. When one can find humor in the very thing meant to suppress them, it weakens the oppressor's impact. For instance, during various oppressive regimes, underground comics, and satirical plays served as subtle revolts, chipping away at the stone facades of tyrants.

Moreover, humor's role in Stoicism—a philosophy deeply concerned with personal virtue and wisdom as the path to true happiness—provides us with profound insights. Stoic philosophers, like Seneca and Epictetus, recognized that humor can be a safeguard against the cruelties of the world. They believed that by adopting a certain light-heartedness, we could distance ourselves from misfortunes, viewing them more as the natural course of life rather than personal affronts. This distancing allows us not only to cope with hardships but to confront them with a composed mind and even a smirk. The Stoics saw humor as a philosophy in its own right—a way to cultivate resilience and maintain equanimity in the face of life's trials.

As we step into this chapter, we'll uncover the myriad ways humor has been both a balm for the soul and a tool of defiance. Through the lens of historical events, philosophical teachings, and everyday resilience, we'll come to understand that even in the most harrowing scenarios, our incredible species finds a way to laugh, and in that laughter, lies our unwavering strength.

Stoicism: It's Not Just About Keeping Your Face Tight

The word 'stoic' often conjures an image of a stern, unsmiling individual braving the harsh winds of life without a flinch. Think of the classic British mantra, "Keep Calm and Carry On," but maybe with a tad less emphasis on the 'calm' part and more on the 'carry on without so much as an eyebrow twitch' approach.

However, this stiff-upper-lip caricature is just that—a caricature. If Stoicism were a person, it would probably roll its eyes at this misrepresentation, followed by a chuckle at the irony of it all. Maybe even a snarky, "Well, that's not very Stoic of you."

Stoicism, as a philosophy, is less about bottling up emotions and more about understanding and dealing with them rationally. It's about recognizing that life, with all its twists, turns, and occasional pies in the face, is as unpredictable as a cat on catnip. While most think Stoics are like the grumpy cat meme—perpetually unamused—they are, in reality, more akin to someone who, after slipping on a banana peel, gets up, dusts themselves off, and remarks, "Well, wasn't that a-peel-ing?" Stoics of the past would love dad jokes. I think.

A significant tenet of Stoicism is observing life just as it is, and that includes the funny and absurd. Stoics believe in aligning with nature and reality, and let's be honest, nature has its own sense of humor. For example, there is absolutely no reason a relatively harmless tarantula should look like that. Please stop it, evolution.

Epictetus, a Stoic heavyweight, pointed out the transience and changeable nature of life, saying, "It's not things that upset us, but our judgment about things." That's ancient wisdom's way of saying, "Don't cry over spilled milk—unless, of course, you slip in it. Then you should laugh because dairy, my friend, isn't supposed to be that dramatic."

I will argue that humor is Stoicism in action. It's the ability to stand back, observe a situation, see the inherent absurdity, and laugh about it. This is the Stoic's version of 'rolling with the punches'—and maybe cracking a joke or two about how they didn't see that left hook coming. Life, in all its unpredictability, throws us curveballs, but it also throws us comedic fodder. The Stoics recognized this. They saw the universe as a place of cosmic irony, where sometimes, you're the statue being shit on, and sometimes, you're the pigeon doing the shitting. Either way, it's quite the hilarious scene.

So, next time you imagine a Stoic, don't picture a robot-like figure who's mastered the Milan Fashion Week runway stare. Instead, envision someone who's able to laugh at the unpredictability of life, knowing that in every misstep, there's a punchline waiting to be delivered. In the words of Marcus Aurelius, "Very little is needed to make a happy life; it is all within yourself, in your way of thinking." And perhaps, just perhaps, that 'little' he mentioned includes a sprinkle of humor, a dash of wit, and a hearty knee slap at the universe's comedic timing.

The Healing Power of Humor: Why Laughter Truly is the Best Medicine

Humor is sometimes regarded as no more than a source of amusement, but that is a superficial perception. It serves as an essential companion during life's turbulent rides, offering refuge, building bridges, and healing wounds. And it's not just me believing these things, it's science.

Coping with Stress and Adversity

There's an old adage that life is what happens when you're busy making other plans. I hate that adage, but even I have to admit it's a real thing. As challenges unexpectedly rear their heads, humor acts as a cushion, softening the blow. Studies have repeatedly demonstrated that laughter reduces cortisol levels – our body's primary stress hormone. One study from Loma Linda University found that even the mere anticipation of laughter can reduce cortisol levels by a staggering 39%. In a practical sense, this means that when faced with adversities, those armed with a sense of humor are biologically better equipped to handle them. Remember that time you missed the bus, only to end up having an unexpected, hilarious adventure on foot? Embracing the lighter side of challenges can transform mishaps into memorable tales.

Building Social Bonds

Humans, at their core, are social beings. Navigating social dynamics, however, isn't always easy. A humorous remark or shared joke can effortlessly break barriers, bridging divides. Researchers from University College London found that shared laughter synchronizes the brain activity of both the speaker and the listener, leading to increased bonding and understanding. It's no wonder that inside jokes often act as the foundation of many long-lasting friendships. That time you and a stranger laughed over a monkey's audacious theft of a full, uneaten, ham sandwich? Bam, instant camaraderie.

Boosting Physical Health and Endorphins

Laughter's benefits are not merely mental or emotional. The physical ramifications of laughter are also in our scientific record. A study from the University of Maryland Medical Center drew a connection between laughter and the healthy function of blood vessels. Laughter gets the blood flowing, comparable to the effect of a workout on the cardiovascular system. When it comes to endorphins, the body's homemade pick-me-ups, a good laugh acts as a catalyst. Researchers from Oxford University found that laughter increases our pain threshold by releasing these very endorphins. Essentially, the old saying of "laugh until it hurts" might be backwards; it's more like "laugh so it doesn't hurt." See what I did there?

Cognitive Reappraisal and Perspective Taking

Humor's real strength lies in its ability to pivot our viewpoint, making us see the mundane in a fresh, often ridiculous, light. Cognitive reappraisal, a psychological tool where individuals reframe their perspective on a situation, is at the core of many humor-induced epiphanies. A study from the University of California, Berkeley, underscores this by demonstrating how humor aids in reframing situations, thus reducing negative emotional responses. For instance, locked out of your house? You've just been handed a prime opportunity for some impromptu stargazing.

An Antidote to Despair

Life can sometimes feel like an uphill battle, especially during periods of profound upheaval. Here, humor can be a candlelight, guiding us through dark times. Viktor Frankl, a Holocaust survivor and psychiatrist, often remarked on the therapeutic effect of humor, even in concentration camps. He noted that a humorous perspective could provide psychological distance from despair, offering a brief respite.

While humor might appear frivolous to many people, it's a powerful, multifaceted tool that has been evolutionarily honed to aid us. Whether it's the bonding laughter shared among friends, the stress relief after a well-timed joke, or the reframe of a challenging situation, humor stands tall as an indispensable ally. As we navigate life's ebbs and flows, especially during trying times, let us remember the potent power of laughter, our built-in defense mechanism, and healer.

Historical Examples of Humor as Resistance

While I want to tread respectfully in the next sections, recognizing the gravity of the situations I am writing about, it's also essential to recognize the power of humor and the resilience it represents. There are moments in our history where we saw a side of humanity that was unequivocally evil, where we caused inconceivable suffering to others.

But even in these times, humor played a pivotal role as an instrument of resistance, a weapon wielded against oppressors, and a lifeline for the oppressed. The dark humor that has arisen during some of the bleakest periods in human history elevates us, and speaks to a refusal to break, a rejection of oppression, and a determination to hold on to our own fundamental human dignity.

Concentration Camps During the Holocaust

The Holocaust, one of the darkest chapters of human history, paradoxically saw moments where humor acted as a guardrail of hope. In the camps, where death and despair were everyday realities, humor was a subversive tool and a mechanism to maintain sanity. In an environment as bleak and terrifying as the concentration camps, humor became an embodiment of resistance. It wasn't just about making someone laugh; it was a silent protest against the degradation of humanity, a middle finger in the face of the oppressor. The humor here wasn't a dismissal of the situation but rather an affirmation of life in the midst of pervasive and needless death.

One story revolves around the renowned therapist, Viktor Frankl. In the face of desolation, Frankl and his companions would attempt to find humor in their situation. He recalls joking with a fellow prisoner, “Be careful, don’t lose weight; you are getting too thin. You might disappear entirely!” Another instance involves a man who, before his execution, sarcastically commented about the bumbling inefficiency of his captors, suggesting they'd probably "botch the hanging."

Jim Crow Era and Black Humorists

During the Jim Crow era, Black Americans were subjected to violent racism and profound social injustices. Yet, humor emerged as an essential tool for resistance and commentary. Black humorists and comedians played a pivotal role in highlighting the absurdities and brutalities of racial segregation and prejudice. The systemic racism and profound social injustices of the Jim Crow era were formidable, yet they could not suppress the vibrant humor that emerged from Black communities. This humor was not merely for entertainment; it was a powerful tool for resistance and a means to illuminate the sheer absurdity of racial prejudice.

One notable example is Moms Mabley, one of the first major Black stand-up comedians, who would often use humor to critique racial discrimination. In one of her acts, she exclaimed,

"You know the best years of my life were spent in the arms of another woman's husband? Yes, dear, Father."

Black comedians wielded humor as both a shield and a sword. Comedy became a stage for challenging prevailing prejudices, questioning established norms, and promoting understanding. Legends like Dick Gregory and Moms Mabley paved the way, employing humor as their weapon against bigotry. Their trailblazing efforts carved out a space for Black voices in comedy to spotlight the deep-seated issues in society.

Soviet Satire and Dissidents

The authoritarian grip of the Soviet regime saw stringent censorship laws and crackdowns against any form of dissent. Yet, satire and humor became popular tools among dissidents to critique the government and its policies. The repressive nature of the Soviet regime stifled freedom of expression, yet humor blossomed as a means of silent rebellion. Soviet citizens utilized wit to navigate the intricacies of life under an authoritarian regime, transforming everyday struggles into sources of laughter and connection.

An anecdote, often whispered among citizens, went like this: "Is it true that the Soviet Union is the most progressive society? Yes, when New York sleeps, Moscow is already at work; when Paris has lunch, Moscow is already at work; and when Beijing finishes work, Moscow is still at work." Another popular joke underscored the dire economic situation: "They pretend to pay us, and we pretend to work."

These jokes, while seemingly light-hearted, carried potent critiques of the Soviet regime and the realities its citizens faced.

They became a means to communicate shared frustrations and aspirations for a more just and hopeful society.

Reflecting on Humor as Resistance Through History

Such instances highlight how humor transcends borders and regimes, acting as a universal language of resistance and defiance. The humor that emerged from these historical precedents wasn't about trivializing real human suffering. It was about finding humanity amidst inhumanity. In the vast uncertainties of collapse, this humor can serve as a guidepost, encouraging us to confront despair with defiance, and darkness with the enduring light of laughter.

Throughout our history, communities that faced the worst forms of oppression often found solace and strength in shared moments of laughter. One might wonder, how is it that individuals, when subjected to the gravest of injustices, find the capacity to laugh? The answer lies in the essence of humor itself. Humor can be more than a spontaneous reaction to a funny incident; it is a deliberate choice, an act of rebellion against the forces that seek to subdue the spirit.

The beauty of such humor lies in its duality. On the surface, it provides a momentary escape from the bleakness of reality. But on a deeper level, it serves as a profound act of resistance. Every joke shared, every laughter echoed becomes a metaphorical raised fist, an affirmation in the face of debilitating subjugation

For societies staring at the abyss of collapse, the lessons from these historical moments are invaluable. Collapse, in many ways, brings with it a sense of loss - a loss of the familiar, a loss of security, a loss of the future we envisioned. Amidst such profound uncertainties, humor becomes a lifeboat. It offers us the chance to navigate the choked waters of hopelessness, helping us find solace in shared experiences and in the collective memory of humanity's resilience.

Moreover, humor, with its inherent capacity to highlight the absurdities of life, can act as a lens, helping societies recognize the follies that led them to the brink of collapse. It can serve as a critique, challenging the prevailing narratives and fostering a culture of introspection and change. Every jest, every satire becomes a mirror, reflecting the flaws and paving the way for transformation.

For parents and caregivers guiding the next generation through these weird times, understanding the value of humor is crucial. It is not about shielding our young ones from the grim realities but equipping them with a tool that has historically proven its merit. By sharing stories, anecdotes, and jokes from the past, we can inspire our children to face the future with a blend of realism and stoicism. As we navigate the uncertainties of collapse, let us remember that humor is a legacy, handed down to us by generations who faced unthinkable adversities yet refused to be defeated. It is a weapon that has protected us in the darkest chapters of history. And as we stand at this pivotal juncture, we must harness the power of humor, using it not simply as a means to cope but as a weapon to defy, to resist, and to rebuild.

The Double Edge of Dark Humor

Dark humor, with its ability to tread the thin line between painful reality and comedic relief, has always possessed an ambiguous nature. It's like walking on the edge of a blade, where on one side lies the therapeutic release of pent-up emotions, and on the other, the precipice of insensitivity and potential harm. This duality makes it one of the most powerful yet perilous tools in the comedic arsenal.

Dark humor finds its roots in the heart of human suffering, drawing out laughs from subjects that, under any other lens, would be deemed tragic or taboo. This very act of defiance against the normative can be empowering. In times of collective trauma or societal upheaval, dark jokes can act as a collective sigh of relief, allowing communities to process their emotions, if only for a fleeting moment. It is cathartic, serving as a safety valve to release the pressures of anguish and despair, reminding us of our shared human fragility.

Yet, this very strength is also its vulnerability. What offers solace and understanding to one might be a painful trigger to another. The boundaries of dark humor are not universal; they are deeply personal, intricately woven with individual experiences, cultural backgrounds, and personal traumas. Consequently, a joke that might seem innocuous to one can deeply wound another.

The Charlie Hebdo massacre is a horrible testament to this reality. In 2015, the French satirical weekly newspaper became the epicenter of a global debate on freedom of expression, religious sensitivity, and the boundaries of humor. The publication, known for its sharp, often controversial cartoons, was targeted in a deadly attack that left many of its staff dead.

The cartoons, particularly those depicting the Prophet Muhammad, were deemed blasphemous by many in the Muslim community. While Charlie Hebdo saw its work as a continuation of the French tradition of satirical critique, many others saw it as a blatant disregard for religious sentiments.

This incident serves as a shocking reminder that humor, particularly of the darker kind, does not exist in a vacuum. It interacts with societal dynamics, power structures, and deeply ingrained beliefs. While the proponents of Charlie Hebdo championed the cause of free speech and the right to satirize, critics questioned the ethics of punching down, especially in a climate of increasing Islamophobia in Europe.

The Charlie Hebdo incident underscores the crux of the challenge with dark humor: determining who gets to decide the line of acceptability. Is it the comedian, drawing from their personal reservoir of experiences and beliefs? Or is it the audience, each member coming with their own set of values and triggers? Or perhaps, is it society at large, with its ever-evolving norms and moral compass?

As we grapple with these questions, especially in an era marked by heightened sensitivities and polarization, it becomes imperative to approach dark humor with a sense of responsibility. This does not mean curtailing the freedom to jest or satirize. Rather, it is about being cognizant of the impact such humor can have, especially on marginalized or vulnerable communities. It is about recognizing that while humor can be a powerful tool for resistance, it can also be weaponized to further entrench prejudices and stereotypes.

Moreover, with everyone grappling with the looming shadow of profound disruption, where traumas are fresh and wounds are raw, the responsibility becomes even more pronounced. The need for laughter is more profound than ever, but so is the need for empathy and understanding. The line between catharsis and insensitivity becomes even thinner, requiring a delicate balance between offering relief and causing harm.

The ambiguous nature of dark humor is both its strength and its challenge. It can act as a salve, healing the soul and offering a respite from the harshness of reality. But it can also sting, reopening old wounds and causing fresh ones. As we navigate this delicate terrain, let us do so with an awareness of its power, harnessing its potential for healing while being wary of its capacity to harm.

Humor as Community Building

In the shared heartbeat of a collective laugh, strangers can become friends, walls can crumble, and bridges can be built. Humor, in its myriad forms, has a unique ability to foster connections, enabling disparate groups to find common ground and celebrate shared experiences. In times of turmoil and uncertainty, humor's role as a tool for community building becomes even more pronounced, transforming laughter from a mere reaction to a fundamental social act.

Bridging Strangers

Humor has an innate ability to bring people together, regardless of their backgrounds, beliefs, or experiences. Take the global reach of a good joke, meme, or viral video, for instance. Something funny can spread across continents, languages, and cultures, proving that our sense of humor often transcends our differences. A joke shared in a subway in New York can resonate with a farmer in rural India or a teacher in South Africa. These moments of shared laughter demonstrate how humor can act as a universal language, knitting together a fragmented planet and reminding us of our shared humanity.

Building Resilience

Shared humor, especially during trying times, fosters resilience. It offers a brief reprieve from the burdens of the day, allowing individuals to recharge emotionally and mentally. Furthermore, sharing a laugh in the face of adversity can signal a collective refusal to be defeated. Historically, oppressed communities have used humor as a coping mechanism, demonstrating an indomitable spirit that refuses to be crushed. Laughter in such contexts isn't an escape from reality but a testament to the human spirit's endurance.

Offering New Perspectives

Satire and parody, a specific form of humor, can shed light on societal flaws and contradictions, challenging the status quo and encouraging introspection. Through the medium of comedy, individuals are often more receptive to new ideas, seeing the world through a different lens and possibly reshaping their beliefs. Comedians and humorists, by presenting familiar situations in an exaggerated or absurd light, can spark dialogues that might have been otherwise challenging to initiate.

A Communal Experience of Joy and Love

While the act of laughing is individual, the experience of humor is often communal. Numerous cultures around the globe have traditions where people gather expressly for the purpose of sharing jokes and laughter. In India, for example, "hasya kavi sammelans" are gatherings where poets recite humorous verses, evoking bouts of laughter from the audience. In Nigeria, "tales by moonlight" often incorporate elements of humor, where elders tell tales to younger generations, fostering a sense of community and shared heritage.

Such traditions underscore the power of communal humor to foster bonds of love, respect, and mutual understanding. In these spaces, laughter becomes an act of communion, a shared experience that nurtures community spirit. In the modern era, this sense of communal joy finds expression in comedy clubs, online meme communities, and even impromptu gatherings where friends and strangers bond over shared jokes and humorous anecdotes.

Humor's role in community building is profound. In an increasingly angry and divided society, the ability to laugh together, to find commonality in humor, becomes an end in itself. It reminds us that even in the darkest times, there is room for joy, love, and connection. As we navigate the uncertainties of the future, let us not underestimate the power of a shared laugh to heal, connect, and inspire. Humor can be the glue that binds us, reinforcing the ties of community and reminding us that we've been doing this laughing thing since the beginning.

Laughter: My Global Passport

Throughout my travels, I've found myself in countries and cities where I was a total and complete outsider. I used to assume that these circumstances would isolate me, creating barriers that might be hard to breach. But that's never been my real lived experience, and there's a simple reason why: the power of gut-busting, hysterical, all-night laughter.

I've always believed that humor, in its purest form, transcends language, culture, and borders. In every new town, I looked to find jokes, humor, and those moments of shared laughter that crush linguistic barriers. There's a universal language, one that doesn't need words — just smartass half-baked cracks.

On countless nights, I've found myself in dimly lit bars or bustling restaurants in a foreign country, surrounded by locals, with whom I shared no formal language. The challenge of effective verbal communication was evident, but instead of feeling alienated, I felt profoundly connected. We would exchange smiles, gestures, and occasionally, through a mix of broken phrases and exaggerated expressions, attempt jokes. As the night progressed, these attempts would lead to genuine moments of hilarity, causing waves of laughter in myself and my new best friends.

On one particular night in a small Estonian town, I remember gesturing wildly to describe something funny that had happened earlier that day. Although the specifics of the story might have been lost in translation, the humor wasn't. My pub friends of locals responded with their own stories, each more animated than the last. Though the words were a jumbled mystery to me, their laughter was clear as day. We used our hands, our bodies, and our phones to help, but by the end of the evening, it felt as though we had shared a lifetime of memories. At one point, a Norwegian guy fully fell off his stool laughing, and hell, that started a brand new bout of hysteria.

Experiences like that have affirmed my belief in the unifying power of humor. Even in places where I couldn't communicate in the traditional sense, I never felt alone. The resonating sound of collective laughter made me feel at home, making strangers feel like old friends. These moments of shared mirth have been my passport, allowing me to connect, understand, and feel a part of communities far removed from my own. They make clear the universal nature of humor, its power to bridge divides, and its ability to create bonds that are as resilient as they are heartwarming.

Raising Our Kids with a Sense of Humor: Why and How

Importance of Instilling a Sense of Humor

Our kids are going to face a lot of bullshit in their lives, marked by uncertainties, change, and challenges. Equipping our children with a sense of humor is more than just a delightful accessory; it's an essential survival tool. It allows them to face adversity with resilience, navigate complexities with ease, and transform potentially overwhelming situations into manageable ones. A sense of humor provides a protective armor against the unavoidable hardships without hardening one's heart.

Building Emotional Resilience: Just as we teach our children the value of perseverance and determination, a sense of humor is another tool in their emotional toolkit. It helps them bounce back from setbacks, looking at challenges not as insurmountable obstacles but as temporary hurdles, often accompanied by a laugh or two.

Encouraging Perspective: Laughter often comes from recognizing the absurdity in situations. This same recognition can help children distance themselves from immediate stressors, allowing them to see the bigger picture and not get bogged down by transient issues.

Promoting Social Connection: Having a sense of humor aids social interactions. It makes one approachable, relatable, and can diffuse tense situations. It's a bridge to understanding others and being understood.

Concrete Actions to Cultivate Humor

Instilling a sense of humor is not about teaching kids to tell jokes, but about creating an environment where laughter is valued, absurdities are celebrated, and lightness prevails even in heavy moments.

Shared Laughing Moments: Dedicate a portion of the day for sheer silliness. Whether it's reading a funny story, watching a short comedic clip, or simply making faces at each other, these moments become daily reminders that it's okay to let go and laugh.

Encourage Curiosity about Humor: Like any other interest, humor can be explored and deepened. Encourage kids to ask why something is funny, delving into the anatomy of a joke or humorous situation. This promotes not just laughter but an understanding of humor.

Practice Lightness in Difficult Times: Whenever there's a minor setback—a spilled glass of milk, a missed bus—use it as an opportunity to make light of the situation. Teach them to appreciate the situation by addressing it with a lighter heart.

Storytelling with a Twist: Children love stories, and adding humorous elements can make them more engaging. Allow kids to come up with their own absurd endings or funny characters, promoting creativity and humor simultaneously.

Participate in Play: Play is the language of children, and it's inherently filled with moments of joy, laughter, and humor. By engaging in play, you can bond with your child and also instill the idea that adulthood doesn't mean the end of fun and laughter.

Lead by Example: Children are keen observers. When they see adults in their life approach situations with humor and lightness, they imbibe the same. Share funny anecdotes from your day, laugh at your own mistakes, and show them that humor is a lifelong companion.

In this absurd time, filled with unpredictable shifts and challenges, humor emerges as a stabilizing force. It's not just about fleeting moments of laughter but about crafting a mindset that can perceive light even in the darkest corners. By fostering a sense of humor in our children, we're handing a shield against life's adversities and we're giving them a lens that can transform bleakness into landscapes filled with silliness and possibility.

For our children, every hearty laugh is a step toward building an inner sanctuary—a place they can retreat to when the outside world gets overwhelming. But the benefits of humor stretch far beyond personal solace. It's a unifying thread that can bridge misunderstandings, connect hearts, and make even the unfamiliar feel like home. By sharing a joke or a funny anecdote, barriers dissolve, and strangers can momentarily become friends.

As parents, our role goes beyond teaching our children how to read, write, or solve math problems. It's also about helping them navigate the vast emotional landscape of life. And in this journey, humor can be their steady companion. It reminds them that every problem has multiple perspectives, that every situation—even the most dire—has a hidden facet that can be approached with a smile. It teaches them adaptability, resilience, and most importantly, the invaluable skill of not carrying life's burdens too heavily.

By fostering a humorous perspective in our children, we're preparing them for a future that is certain to be riddled with complexities and bullshit. But with humor by their side, they'll be equipped to tackle challenges head-on, turning stumbling blocks into stepping stones. They'll learn the art of bouncing back, of seeing the comedic lining, and of finding joy in the smallest things. And as they grow, this perspective will become their strength, helping them create pockets of happiness, irrespective of the external circumstances.

The legacy of laughter is perhaps one of the most profound gifts we can give our children. It's a reminder that even in the face of profound uncertainty, there's always a reason to smile, always an angle that beckons joy. By instilling this in our young ones, we're not just brightening their present but also lighting up their path for their years to come.

6: The Hardest Job We Will Ever Have

"You become responsible, forever, for what you have tamed."

-***The Little Prince* by Antoine de Saint-Exupéry**

As the world I once knew begins to unravel in its entirety, and the first glows of a new and unknowable day emerge, I find myself caught between moments of profound loss and unexplored potential. For all of us, and particularly for parents, this is more than a moment of transition, it's now a rite of passage. No parent will be untouched by this. The fabric of society is undergoing a seismic shift, and in the midst of this, we parents are entrusted with a task unparalleled in its significance: guiding the next generation through the labyrinth.

Many of us grew up with dreams of what parenting might look like — the idyllic moments, the milestones, the shared joys, and even the inevitable challenges. But none of us could have fully envisioned this unique juncture, where our roles as parents are about pioneering a path through uncharted territories. Yet, here we are, holding the torches of resilience, wisdom, and maybe even a little hope. Amidst the chaos and uncertainty, we've taken on what is undoubtedly the hardest job we'll ever have. It's a role that demands constant evolution, boundless patience, and an unwavering commitment to the future. And as I reflect on my own journey and the countless moments of doubt and determination, I find solace in knowing that I'm not alone. Across the globe, parents are rising to this challenge, each carving out their own path, each lighting the way for others.

I write this not just as an observer but as a fellow traveler, having dedicated myself wholly to the monumental role of parenting in this unprecedented time. It is a commitment that is as daunting as it is grounding. There are moments of heart-wrenching sorrow, where the weight of it all seems too much to hold. But there are also moments of profound joy, where the simplest gesture — a child's laugh, a shared song, or a quiet conversation — reminds us of the incomparable beauty of human connection.

To my fellow parents, I offer both compassion and camaraderie, and this is my call. Our journey is fraught with challenges, and the road ahead is long and uncertain. But together, we must stand defiantly against the tide of despair, anchored by our shared purpose and unwavering love for our children. We are the custodians of the future, the tree truck that provides support, and the canopy that offers shade on a rapidly changing and degrading planet.

With our clear-eyed look at our future we must remind ourselves that this is not simply about survival, this is about legacy. It's about the stories we tell, the lessons we impart, and the hearts we shape for those who come after us. We are laying the foundations for a new time, one where the values of resilience, creativity, and introspection will illuminate the road.

So, as we embark on this journey, let us stand tall and resolute, hand in hand, heart to heart. The challenges we face are immense, but our collective strength and determination is even greater. This is our moment, and together, we will rise to meet it, because we absolutely must. For us parents living through today, we simultaneously meet the end of our old way of life, and the beginning of a new way, one we define for ourselves by our actions, our choices, and our unwavering commitment to the future.

The Cosmic Rarity of Life

Almost all planets in the universe will form and be swallowed by their dying star, never experiencing life at all. Think about that for a moment. With billions upon billions of celestial bodies out there, most will never know the pulse of a heartbeat, the warmth of sunlight filtered through an atmosphere, or the intricate dance of complex and beautiful ecosystems.

Now, contrast that with our peculiar situation on Earth. By some cosmic twist of fate, we find ourselves on this life-rich planet, bursting with a diverse array of species, climates, and landscapes. Our blue planet isn't just another rock floating in space; it's a living, breathing entity, with us as one of its most cognizant inhabitants. The odds of our existence, when looked at in the grand scheme of things, are mind-bogglingly slim. It's as if the universe rolled the dice trillions of times, and we were the one roll that won everything. This isn't about getting philosophical; it's about recognizing the sheer mathematical improbability of our situation and celebrating it.

Being alive is far from straightforward. It's filled with challenges, setbacks, joys, and sorrows. There are days when the weight of existence can feel overwhelming, and the complexities of life make us question the very essence of our being. Yet, when all is said and done, the very fact that we have the privilege to question, to feel, to experience—to live—is pretty damn extraordinary.

Some might argue it's double-edged, this thing called life, and perhaps, in many ways, they're right. But isn't there something defiantly wonderful about our very existence? In a universe so vast, where life is the exception and not the norm, we get to be part of the select few who can say, "We lived."

The Beautiful Cruelty of Mortality

Mortality is the ultimate conundrum. It's a strange and uncomfortable truth: the heartbeat that grants us life is also counting down to its eventual silence. How does one make peace with that? I often find myself caught in the enormity of this contradiction, grappling with the idea of an endpoint to my consciousness, my emotions, my memories. It feels, at times, as if the universe has dealt us a cruel hand, giving us the gift of life only to reclaim it in the end.

Yet, the deeper I dive into this introspection, the clearer it becomes that the real cruelty would be in not recognizing the profound beauty of our transitory existence. Mortality, with all its intricacies, is what amplifies the value of each moment we live. It is the stark backdrop against which the vibrancy of our lives plays out.

We humans, ever since our early days huddled around fires in dark caves, have tried to confront and conquer the idea of death. We've crafted myths, religions, and stories of afterlives, attempting to find solace in the thought that there might be something beyond this life. But regardless of our beliefs or faith in an eternal soul, one truth remains: our time on this Earth is limited.

Civilizations have risen, touched the clouds with their glory, and then crumbled back into the jungle and sea. But the legacy of humanity isn't defined by our empires or our monuments, it is defined by our collective spirit, our art, our shared tales of love, heroism, sacrifice, and, yes, our shared moments of joy and despair. It's in our nature to cling to life, to rail against the very idea of our end. Yet, it's precisely in embracing our mortality that we can live our lives with the fiercest intensity. By accepting the inescapable dance of life and death, we free ourselves to cherish our time, to revel in our experiences, and to create memories that, in some small way, defy the unstoppable march of time. We're here, living and breathing, and in the infinite darkness of the universe.

The Gift of Now

If we were to lay out the enormity of time against the backdrop of the universe, the present moment, the 'now,' would appear totally insignificant, an inconsequential flash. But it's within this seemingly meaningless flash that the entirety of our existence unfolds. Every feeling, every thought, every action occurs in the moment called now. And while the vast expanse of time might dwarf our present, it is this present that holds a singular power.

The past, with its memories, lessons, and scars, has its place. It shapes us, molds us, teaches us. Yet, it's a place we can never return to, a silent movie we play in our minds. The future is a canvas still blank, filled with abstract dreams, fears, and uncertainties. While it's natural to look forward and plan, the future remains an enigma, its realities completely unknown.

But now? Now is alive. It pulses with energy, potential, and reality. It's the space where life truly happens. Every heartbeat, every breath, every tear, and every laugh emanates from this sacred chamber of the present. And in recognizing this, we unlock an enormous reservoir of potential.

The Buddhist monk Thích Nhất Hạnh said, "Life is available only in the present moment." The past is a memory, and the future is a dream. Yet, we often let the shadows of our yesterdays and the mirages of our tomorrows cloud the vibrant colors of our now. We delay our happiness, thinking there's always a tomorrow. We brood over past mistakes, allowing them to steal the joy of our current moments. But in doing so, we forget a fundamental truth: life unfolds in the present. Embracing the now doesn't just mean being aware of the present; it's about actively engaging with it. It's about immersing oneself in the beauty of a fleeting moment, whether that's the infectious laughter of a child, the delicate aroma of a blooming flower, the warm embrace of a loved one, or the gentle, rhythmic patter of rain against a tin roof. These moments, though they might seem trivial against the vastness of our lives, are where true living happens. They ground us, connect us, and remind us of the raw beauty of existence.

It's easy to feel overwhelmed in our degrading world, with its myriad challenges and unending news feed of doom. Amidst this cacophony, the present offers a sanctuary. It's a potent reminder that while we might not hold the reins to every external event, we absolutely can control our internal selves. We can choose to respond with love rather than react in fear. We can decide to live intentionally, with purpose and passion, cherishing each moment as the precious gift that it is.

And to truly grasp the power of now is to acknowledge and accept its fleeting nature. It's this ephemeral reality that its magic lies. Because when we realize that our moments are numbered, we can begin to treat them with the reverence they deserve. We learn to dance in the rain, skydive out of planes, love with an open heart, and truly live, rather than merely exist.

Our Kids Are Our Hope

Not someone else's kids, not kids unborn, but our kids, right now. They are who will live through this self-inflicted mess, and if there is anything to rebuild, they will be the ones to do so. There is no other realistic plan. This can sound impossible for many, but to us, it stands as a defiant call to action. It may be a future vastly alien from our familiar past, with challenges that we might deem inconceivable, but hear this: we will rise to meet it with unmatched fervor and determination.

I look to Malala Yousafzai, who, with the fearless heart instilled in her by her father, stared down the barrel of extremism and championed the cause of girls' education. Solomon Radasky, a light from one of history's darkest hours, spent his entire life after surviving the Holocaust reminding us that even when faced with the unimaginable, the human spirit can endure and even rise. The Bhagavad Gita, the ancient Hindu text, echoes that with the fierce teachings of duty, righteousness, and the unwavering strength required when looking directly at the unknowable.

Let there be no mistake: we stand united, an unbreakable front against the storm of the future. We will not be subdued. We will not let our children enter this future ill-equipped or fearful. With the strength drawn from our ancestors, the wisdom of time and a fire that will not be extinguished: We are ready. Our children will be more than ready. No matter the magnitude of the challenge, we shall neither falter nor fail. In our hearts and souls lives the tireless spirit of human resilience.

And when it comes to our kids, our defiance will not stutter, not even for a moment.

References Appendix

Gore, Al. An Inconvenient Truth: The Planetary Emergency of Global Warming and What We Can Do About It. Rodale Books, 2006.

Linklater, Richard. Before Sunrise (1995), Before Sunset (2004), and Before Midnight (2013). Castle Rock Entertainment, Detour Filmproduction, et al.

Gawande, Atul. Being Mortal: Medicine and What Matters in the End. Metropolitan Books, 2014.

Lama, Dalai, and Desmond Tutu. The Book of Joy: Lasting Happiness in a Changing World. Avery, 2016.

Levitin, Daniel J. The Organized Mind: Thinking Straight in the Age of Information Overload. Dutton, 2014.

Sagan, Carl. The Demon-Haunted World: Science as a Candle in the Dark. Random House, 1995.

Robinson, Ken. "Schools Kill Creativity." TED Talk, 2006.

Gottschall, Jonathan. The Storytelling Animal: How Stories Make Us Human. Houghton Mifflin Harcourt, 2012.

Frankl, Viktor E. Man's Search for Meaning. Beacon Press, 1959.

Benigni, Roberto. Life Is Beautiful (original title: La Vita è Bella). Miramax, 1997.

Hugo, Victor. The Man Who Laughs. Translated by William Young. D. Appleton and company, 1869.

Scholarly Articles Cited

Berk, L. A., et al. "Neuroendocrine and Stress Hormone Changes during Mirthful Laughter." American Journal of Medical Science, 298.1 (1989): 39-44.

Miller, M., et al. "Laughter Improves Blood Vessel Function and Reduces Stress Reactivity in Healthy Individuals." Journal of the American Medical Association, 301.17 (2009): 1767-1775.

Cousins, Norman. "Laughter and Endorphins: Endogenous Morphine-Like Peptides and Stress." New England Journal of Medicine, 321.11 (1989): 661-664.

Keltner, Dacher, and Sarah A. Haidt. "Humor and Emotional Responses." Psychological Science, 8.1 (1997): 72-76.

Scott, Sophie, et al. "Synchronized Laughter and Its Relationship with Social Bonding." Proceedings of the Royal Society B: Biological Sciences, 280.1765 (2013): 20122469.